Antoine and the Théâtre-Libre

Antoine
and
The Théâtre-Libre

BY

SAMUEL MONTEFIORE WAXMAN

PROFESSOR IN BOSTON UNIVERSITY

BENJAMIN BLOM, INC.

New York

First published by Harvard University Press, 1926
Reissued 1964 by Benjamin Blom, Inc., NY 52
L. C. Catalog Card No.: 63-23192

Printed in U.S.A. by
NOBLE OFFSET PRINTERS, INC.
NEW YORK 3, N. Y.

To

MY FATHER

Foreword

THIS study represents the enlargement in scope of the opening chapters of what was originally planned to be a survey of contemporary French drama, based on a series of lectures given at Harvard University, the Boston Public Library, and Boston University. But a recent sojourn in Paris having opened up a treasure-house of Antoiniana, I have restricted this present work to the beginnings of the modern dramatic movement and to its guiding spirit, Antoine. Moreover, Messrs. Clark, Chandler, and Smith in their books on contemporary French drama have amply covered the larger field.

There is no exhaustive study in English on the Théâtre-Libre, Mr. Clark having confined himself to a short sketch of its history prefacing his translation of *Four Plays of the Free Theater*. My chief printed sources, besides the forty tomes of newspaper clippings found in Antoine's library, are Thalasso's *Théâtre Libre* and Antoine's published diary, *Mes Souvenirs sur le Théâtre-Libre*, the one an excellent and indispensable compilation of data, but in no sense a complete critical survey, the other a valuable collection of anecdotic reminiscences. My unprinted sources, exclusive of those obtained from Antoine himself, are based on conversations with MM. Brieux, Fabre, and Wolff, who wrote plays for the Thé-

âtre-Libre, MM. Gémier, Lugné-Poe, and Mme. Eugénie
Nau, who acted at the Théâtre-Libre, MM. Copeau and
Dullin, twin Antoines of to-day, and MM. Benjamin,
Dubech, Gsell, and Hérold, critics and men of letters.

And here I have the pleasant duty of thanking my old
friend, M. Henri Lemaître, for his unerring guidance to
fields of fruitful research, my new friend, M. Édouard
Champion, whose *Open Sesame* unbarred the gates to the
precious archives of Antoine, and my wife, Frances
Sheafer Waxman, who has acted as my helpful amanu-
ensis, critic, and proof-reader.

As for my debt to Antoine himself — well, I have
written this book about him.

S. M. W.

CAMBRIDGE, MASSACHUSETTS
December 1, 1925

Contents

CHAPTER I

FORERUNNERS OF THE THEATRE–LIBRE

(*The Dog Barks*)

MORE paper has been blackened on the art of the drama than on any other genre of literature. Iconoclasts notwithstanding, the drama has been the most difficult literary citadel to conquer, and the plays of many a famous poet and novelist sleep in the dramatic graveyard of the ages. French literature of the nineteenth century is no exception to this rule, and, among lesser lights, Balzac, Flaubert, the Goncourts, and Zola lie buried there. Whatever may have been their influence on the trend of the drama, these writers have failed to convince either their contemporaries or posterity that they could write great plays.

French dramatists, long under the spell of Aristotelian and pseudo-Aristotelian rules, have had a tendency to over-conventionalize what is by nature the most conventional of literary genres, thus depriving France of a great national tragedy. For to the benighted foreign critic, unblessed with that famous *tête racinienne*, the tragedies of the sixteenth, seventeenth, and eighteenth centuries are neo-Greek and neo-Roman rather than French. Few French critics have been iconoclastic enough to admit such a violent heresy, but among them, Zola and Antoine, who have had more influence on the French drama of the nineteenth century than any other two men, have blasphemed. Yet if France cannot boast of a great national tragedy, she can offer something that no other modern European literature can equal — a long unbroken line of masterpieces of national comedy. A pure Gallic stream has pervaded French comedy from the fifteenth-century *Maître Pathelin* to the contemporary farces of Georges Courteline.

French literary critics, and too many foreign critics taking their cue from the French, have been wont to pay undue attention to schools. The rigidly logical mind of the French has led them into the error of netting writers into fixed literary schools, as if they were so many fish. Authors are often found pigeon-holed into groups in most arbitrary fashion. Many shades of writers would be much happier in their Elysian sojourn were their names removed from this or that school. French dramatic literature of the nineteenth century suffers much from this scholastic mania. It has been conveniently divided into three parts, the romantic, the realist, and the naturalist schools. Since the eruption of the symbolists, neo-romanticists, psychologists, Freudians, dadaists, unanimists, and expressionists, no critic has had the temerity to invent a single all-embracing name. The most drastic pronouncement has been that the drama of contemporary France, being in a state of semi-decadence, is unworthy of a special designation.

To squeeze such antipodal names as Musset and Scribe into the romantic school, as do so many dramatic critics, merely because they wrote when romanticism was in flower, requires a deal of straight-jacketing. These two playwrights can by no Procrustean method be made to sleep in the same dramatic bed. As individuals, they exerted far more influence than true romantic playwrights like Hugo and Dumas père. From these two non-romantic dramatists, Musset and Scribe, flowed the two main currents of the drama of nineteenth-century France. I do not mean to be trapped in my own net by affirming that they founded schools of drama; they merely set the type for two styles of playwriting, the well-constructed play and the loosely constructed play. Scribe regarded technique as the first requisite of the playwright, Musset eschewed technique entirely. Pure romantic drama died childless early in life, of apoplexy brought on by violent fits of anger against the classicists.

There was toward the middle of the century a well-defined reaction against romanticism in all its literary manifestations; but Musset, who has been almost universally classified as a playwright of the romantic school, has been constantly gaining in popularity since his death, and his belated vogue began with the rise of realism. So much for romanticism and realism. Between realism and naturalism there is no sharp line of demarcation, either in the drama or in the other forms of literary expression. Naturalism is merely an exaggerated form of realism. It is a question whether there actually existed a naturalist school of literature. But more of that later.

I am concerned here mainly with only one of the two currents, that one which was set in motion by Musset, the freest of dramatists before the Free Theatre. Alfred de Musset, the playwright, has been treated very cavalierly by most dramatic critics. Petit de Julleville, in his *Histoire du Théâtre Français*, does not mention him at all, and our own Brander Matthews, in his *French Dramatists of the Nineteenth Century*, gives an entire chapter to Octave

Feuillet the playwright, and simply mentions Musset in passing as an immoral influence on the chaste Octave. Even Sainte-Beuve dismisses Musset's plays as charming trifles, and Brunetière the dramatic lawgiver, is not so sure that Musset can be taken seriously as a playwright. But more eclectic spirits, like Musset's contemporary, Gautier, and Jules Lemaître, one of the most open-minded of French critics, have not hesitated to salute him as one of France's greatest dramatic glories. Zola, the iconoclast, has gone so far as to characterize Musset as the foremost French dramatist of the nineteenth century, and French critics of to-day are slowly waking up to the fact that what seemed an exaggeration fifty years ago is fast becoming a commonplace. So far as the general public is concerned, Musset now ranks second in point of popularity, with Molière still in the lead.

During the eighteen-thirties and forties Musset wrote a dozen unclassifiable masterpieces, which are neither romantic nor realist; they are Mussetian, for he himself figures in them all, in varying moods, now comic, now tragic, now playful, now serious, now lyric, now fantastic, but never dull, never theatrical, and, above all, always poetic. There is far more poetry in the prose of Musset's plays than in the verse of the plays of Victor Hugo. After the failure of his first play in 1830, Musset ceased writing plays for the stage — that is, with one eye on the public and the other on the critics. He sent them off to the *Revue des Deux Mondes* without a thought of their adaptability for the boards. Written during the romantic epoch, they did not see the footlights until the time when the realists were supposed to have swept him, the so-called romantic playwright, off the stage.

The story goes that Musset, the dramatist, was discovered by accident, not in France but in Russia. A French actress, M,me. Allan-Despréaux, who was playing in St. Petersburg, saw a little play and asked to have it translated into French. She was told that such a labor would be unnecessary as the original had been written by her compatriot, Musset. On her return to Paris she succeeded in having this play, *Un Caprice*, produced. That took place in 1847, thirteen years after the playlet had been written. Since that year, one after another of Musset's plays have gradually found their way to the stage, and have maintained themselves there, some of them not appearing until long after the poet's death. And yet there are critics who still refer to Musset's plays as closet drama!

There is nothing like Musset's theatre in all French dramatic literature. His plays hold a place apart. In one there may be found a touch of Molière, in another of Marivaux, in yet another of Shakespeare or Schiller, but nowhere is Musset closely imitative. He is as unconcerned with dramatic rules as he is with morals, both of which had for him no place in art. He is the most Elizabethan of all French playwrights, and he was more familiar with English drama than are most French men of letters. His construction is so formless, so arbitrary, so un-Gallic, that he completely disconcerted the orderly minds of his compatriots. His world was a world of dramatic imagination, just as Scribe's was one of material imagination. *Les Caprices de Marianne*, *On ne badine pas avec l'amour*, *Le Chandelier*, *Fantasio*, *Un Caprice*, are so many "delicate pastels," as one French critic has it. Musset created no school, he wrote no prefaces, he had no dramatic theories, but he did free French drama from conventions and rules, romantic as well as classic. And every French dramatist who after his time tried to write free plays, first failed on the stage just like Musset. It was not until after the battles of Zola, Becque, and the Théâtre-Libre that French critics grudgingly accepted the freely constructed play.

About the same time that Musset the playwright was being discovered in Paris, Balzac was making his futile, clumsy attempts to counteract the romantic melodrama and the machine-made play of Scribe. "If Balzac had not been discouraged by an ignorant public, he might have written great plays," says Zola. But after flecking off the dust of oblivion that has collected on Balzac's dramatic works, one finds them dull and heavy. Just as we are unconscious of any premeditated attempt to reform the drama on the part of Musset, so we are conscious in the case of Balzac that he was making a prodigious effort to do something revolutionary. Balzac has absolutely no sense of dramatic dialogue. To be sure, his plays do contain dramatic scenes, as might be expected from the author of *La Comédie humaine*, but they would never have won their *succès d'estime* on the stage had they not been retouched. *Le Faiseur* has not only been reduced from four acts to three, but its name has been changed to *Mercadet*. In this disguised form it appears now on the boards of the Comédie-Française. Balzac *à la Dennery* is just as diluted as Zola *à la Busnach*. The only enduring element in Balzac's play is its characterization of the *faiseur*, Mercadet, thus adding one more portrait to that novelist's gallery. *La Marâtre*, of 1848, is a better piece of work. It is a nineteenth-century realistic version of *Romeo and Juliet*, but lacks the sublime quality of the true dramatic poet. Balzac changes his scene at will in the course of an act and blindly disregards all conventions, yet he fails to improve upon the drama of his contemporaries. The conventionally-minded Sarcey, who saw *La Marâtre* in 1859, hailed it as "the first attempt at a new style of drama. It is awkward and hesitating, but it shows sparks of genius. Hats off, if you please, realism has taken possession of the drama."

Now if literary critics must have schools and dates in which to enclose them, Balzac's *Marâtre* is much more revolutionary than *La Dame aux camélias*, familiar to us under the stupid title, *Camille*. Furthermore, it antedated Dumas's play by one year. *La Marâtre* was produced in 1848. Dumas wrote *La Dame aux camélias* in 1849, but it was not played until 1852. It is merely a modern *Marion Delorme*, Victor Hugo *à la Scribe*. It is more like the swan song of the romanticists than the cradle song of a dramatic revolution.

Zola was one of the first to recognize that Musset and Balzac had completely broken with the traditions of the past and had cleared the ground for the foundation of a new style of playwriting. It was Zola who first claimed Balzac for what he termed the naturalist school of drama. It was he who invented, or rather resuscitated, the modern use of the term naturalism. Two of the greatest forces in contemporary French drama, Becque and Antoine, whose names have been popularly associated with the so-called naturalist school of drama, never liked the term. Neither did the Goncourts nor Flaubert, who have been classed as naturalists, despite their protests, by critics who have come after Zola. Emile Zola reminds one in many respects of Diderot, from whom he claims dramatic descent. Both were more romantic than they believed themselves to be, both exercised a considerable influence on the drama of France, and neither of the two was successful with the public. Beaumarchais and Becque stole the thunder of these two thunderers. To-day Diderot's bust graces the precincts of France's dramatic holy of holies, the Comédie-Française, but Zola is penetrating the high places more slowly. Although his body lies in the Panthéon, his works, imaginative as well as critical, have not yet found their way into the library of the Sorbonne!

"Back to nature," cried Diderot, with the air of having made an original discovery. "Back to nature," echoed Zola a hundred years later. And although they furnished their respective ages with searching æsthetic criticisms, they both confused art, which is a finished product, with nature, which is a raw material. To Zola, Diderot was the father of the naturalist school of drama just as Rousseau was the father of the romantic school, and Balzac was its first exponent. Zola was, of course, exaggerating when he leaped back to Diderot, thus blindly disregarding the dramatic evolution of a century. Balzac had made an attempt to continue the Diderotian type of *tragédie bourgeoise*, which neither the romanticists nor Scribe had followed. But so far as substance is concerned, the so-called naturalist drama merely represents a more violent reaction against the romanticists than does that of the realists. Its real originality consists in combating rules of technique. It favored a loosely constructed drama which, in its exaggerated forms, degenerated into a series of tableaux, but in which characters were not distorted in order that they might fit into certain conventional structural laws.

Dumas fils and Augier might be considered sufficiently ultra-realistic in their later plays, but Zola, self-constituted high priest of the new school, weighed them in the balance and found them both wanting. To Zola, Dumas all but found the true formula, and had begun in the right direction with *La Dame aux camélias*, but he came to be so obsessed with the fervor of the preacher and the teacher that his powers of observation became dulled. He used truth merely as a springboard from which to jump into a void. Then, besides, Dumas was witty, and so he was forthwith cast into dramatic limbo with the pronouncement that no genius was ever witty. Augier found more favor in the eyes of Zola. He brought observation and real life to the stage, but he was too fond of stereotyped stage tricks and conventional characters; he was not forceful and original enough to strike out for himself. He was less brilliant but more human than Dumas. The only praiseworthy element that Zola could find in Sardou, for several decades the dramatic god of the Paris boulevard theatres, was his stage-setting, which was meticulously exact in every detail, and his realistic handling of crowds. But these were, after all, only external affairs. Sardou was but an improved Scribe. Zola accused Scribe of introducing into dramatic criticism that baleful term, *métier*, thus making of the drama a profession and not an art. What did France's greatest dramatist, Molière, know about *métier?* The well-constructed play was to Zola the dramatic toy of all Europe, imported everywhere, like the famous *articles de Paris*. Poor Scribe! His dead body was once more exhumed. Although he had been declining since 1860, he was being constantly offered up during the seventies and eighties as a sacrifice to the new dramatic gods.

But let it be said in Zola's defence that, although Scribe's plays had lost their vogue at the time of Zola's writing, his influence throughout Europe was most potent, and Zola contributed more to demolishing the Scribian technique than any one in or out of France. Nearly half a century has passed since these harsh criticisms of once world-renowned playwrights were cried in the wilderness, and posterity has leaned on the side of Zola. Scribe has never been resuscitated, Sardou is dead, Dumas is moribund, and Augier is the only one of them all who is holding his own with one or two plays still living.

To the average mind the name of Zola connotes something unwholesome and unsavory, a condition for which Zola has only himself to blame. In France to-day, in certain literary and academic circles, it is still considered blasphemous to utter his name. But the unprejudiced critic, who may indeed find a large part of his creative work nauseating, must admit that his private life was conspicuously blameless, and that as an author and critic, as well as in his single political adventure, the Dreyfus affair, he was honest and sincere, although he at times waxed peevish. That he was an extremist in his criticisms as well as in his creative work there is no gainsaying. He strove so hard to swing the pendulum in the opposite direction from that in which it was going that he lost his balance and fell over backward. The violence of his critical judgments, and his frequent unjust charges that his adversaries were not acting in good faith, often defeated his own purpose. His opposition to the romanticists was just as extreme as was theirs to the classicists. And for all his theories, what is Zola but a naturalist bird with romantic feathers? He himself admitted that his generation had been so steeped in the romantic hallucination that it could never hope to shake it off completely. His enemies have not dealt gently with him and have piled abuse upon him alive and dead. We can afford to deal more mercifully with him now that the dust of at least his literary battles has cleared away.

That vague term naturalism, which Zola imposed upon an unwilling world, was neither original nor felicitous. Furthermore, it is ambiguous; it has philosophical, theological, scientific, as well as æsthetic connotations. Zola makes it date from the first line that man wrote. As a matter of fact, it really goes back to Aristotle. It has moreover been used by French critics to designate creative work in arts and letters, now of the seventeenth, now of the eighteenth century. His own epoch Zola insisted was the most favorable to its growth, and he identified the modern movement, which stressed the physical and scorned the metaphysical, with the Greek conception of letters which aimed to imitate nature. He vowed that he did not pretend to box French literature into a single formula and stunt its future development; he was baptizing a movement which, since Balzac and Stendhal, had dominated French literature of the nineteenth century. Just as the literature of the seventeenth century was the daughter of Descartes, and that of the eighteenth the daughter of Rousseau, Voltaire, and Diderot, so the naturalist movement was the progeny of the positivist and scientific philosophy of Taine and Claude Bernard. "We are children of naturalism in all things, in politics as in philosophy, in science as well as in literature and art." To him art necessarily corresponded with social and scientific evolution. And so, borrowing the positivism and determinism of Taine and Bernard as well as the physiological and hereditary theories of Letourneau and Lucas, he proceeded to graft this philosophy of life on to his creative work and to preach it as an æsthetic formula. His oft-quoted definition of art as "a corner of nature seen through a temperament" became a sort of war-cry of his followers.

Zola found himself in agreement with certain unnamed foreign critics, who expressed their astonishment that as late as 1880 there should be two distinct literatures in France, the novel and the drama. What he probably meant was that he was bitterly disappointed to find that, although he had been recognized as the standard-bearer of the naturalist novel, he had been unsuccessful in establishing himself as chief of a dramatic school of naturalism, either as a playwright or as a critic. Zola writes with all the fervor of a crusader going to do battle with the literary infidels. The drama was the last stronghold of literary conventionalism, which was to be captured at all costs. To the consternation of Sarcey and others to whom Dumas and Augier were little less than gods, he claimed that in 1879 the French stage was a void. To him Sarcey was but a *lundiste*, a newspaper chronicler, whereas he himself was a dramatic philosopher who surveyed the drama as a whole. Once French plays had lifelike characters moving in a false background; in his day they had naught but false characters moving in a lifelike background. That is, the classic drama did portray man in the abstract, but it was mainly oratorical. As for the romantic drama, it was a purely negative affair; it proclaimed the liberty of dramatic art, but it created nothing. The romantic school merely replaced one form of rhetoric with another which was its inferior. Furthermore, both classic and romantic formulas were based upon an idealized man and were therefore untrue to life. Both schools built their works upon all kinds of philosophical and religious prejudices, under the pretext that the unknown was more noble and more beautiful than the known.

To Zola's way of thinking, the literary naturalist was just as much of a scientist as the biologist or the chemist, and he never tired of quoting from his scientific bible, Bernard's *Introduction to Experimental Medicine*. The naturalist should dissect the human soul and put the results of his investigations into his novels and plays. He must be a strict observer of facts, those "little significant facts" which Taine extolled and with which Zola and his contemporaries filled their notebooks. The writer should never preach, he should restrict himself to stating facts exactly as he found them. Just as Bernard claimed that the scientist was a judge of nature, so Zola claimed that the author should sit in the seat of justice and pass judgments upon man and his deeds of passion. He is not a judge of what is right and wrong, however; he should always remain coldly impersonal. "Vice and virtue," he quotes from Taine, "are products like sugar and vitriol." A writer should not sympathize with his victims. One cannot conceive of a scientist getting angry with nitrogen because it is harmful to life, or having a fondness for oxygen which is beneficial to it. In short, naturalism was applied science. The play or the novel of the naturalist, instead of being a mere amusement for the indolent or a romantic illusion for the idealist, would become a scientific study of man, a study which was still in its infancy. The man of letters would then be conferring a boon upon humanity by working hand in hand with the scholar in the laboratory, and might even go in advance of him in the experimental study of the unknown.

The naturalist school was but the modern development of seventeenth-century classicism. It would be more true to life since modern man was being studied in the light of recent scientific discoveries and placed in his proper environment. Man had ceased to be the mere abstraction that he was in the classic period of French literature. Zola admitted that the novel of the nineteenth century seemed to have replaced the play of the seventeenth century, but he prophesied that the drama would have its day, and he claimed that novelists like Balzac, Stendhal, Flaubert, and the Goncourts, were giving the public a taste of naturalism which would make it sicken of the insipid plays upon which it had been feeding.

Zola is honest enough to quote Bernard's arguments against his cherished literary theories. To Bernard literature is purely creative and in it personality dominates everything else. A literary work is to him a spontaneous creation which has nothing in common with scientific phenomena. But Zola brushes these statements aside, and begs the question by affirming that Bernard was probably thinking of lyric poets when he penned those words. Never would he have set down such heresies had he had Balzac and Stendhal in mind.

In Zola's ideal play there would be no romantic yearnings, no poetic outpourings. Man would be analyzed scientifically and placed in his true environment, which should be staged just as minutely as it is described in the novel. To him the drama of his contemporaries was primarily a question of equilibrium and symmetry, it was neither art nor literature. Plays were put together just like the parts of a watch, and the dramatist was nothing but a clever watchmaker. Zola was for abolishing every convention previously known to the drama. Exposition, intrigue, dénouement were entirely unnecessary. For the drama of invention and imagination, he would substitute a drama of observation and scientific fact. To write a play, a dramatist need only reproduce on the stage the story of a person or a group of persons taken from real life. This story might not be complete, it might be simply a *lambeau d'existence*. Jean Jullien merely paraphrased Zola's *fragment of existence* when he characterized this type of play as a *tranche de vie*. And thus it was that a *slice of life* became the battle-cry of the free dramatists of the Théâtre-Libre. The *personnage sympathique* was not to be replaced by the *personnage antipathique*. "Only the imbeciles accuse me of that," continued Zola, who proposed only to eliminate the conventional character, whose psychology was distorted in order that he might win the sympathy of the audience. To Zola the drama was suffering from the pathetic fallacy. Characters in a play should be neither eloquent nor witty, they should not invoke laughter or tears, or even applause. "Our drama will be naturalist or it will not be," he thundered.

Zola had a word to say on all matters pertaining to dramatic production. He objected to wings and back-drops. He prophesied that footlights would be eventually abandoned. He opposed the stereotyped manner of acting taught at the *Conservatoire* and the playing up to the audience for effects. He was very severe with actresses who distorted the environment of their characters with their lavish display of gowns. He prophesied that within fifty

years from the time that he wrote, all his theories and reforms would be accepted. Forty-odd years have now
passed and certainly almost all the changes advocated by
him have been adopted, not only in France, but throughout the whole dramatic world. By the time that the full
half-century has passed, the last scenic convention, the
footlights, will have disappeared.

There are grains of æsthetic criticism in Zola's pronun-
ciamentoes on playwriting. To be sure, he exaggerated
the importance of Scribe's influence, and in his passionate
opposition to the well-constructed play, he offered in ex-
change an amorphous series of tableaux. To him every
dramatic tradition must go by the board merely because
a new age must have a totally new formula. But he was so
obsessed with his scientific mania, and was so permeated
with the novelist's point of view, that some of his criticisms have fallen flat. Other critics since his day have ex-
tracted the quintessence of his theories, toned down his
overstatements, and reaped the glory that is rightfully
his. Zola lacked *sophrosuné*, that highly prized characteristic of the Greeks, the balance and self-restraint which is
the measure of all true critics. Those who do not belong to
the dogmatic school of critics and who have read the
Spanish *Celestina* and the English *Dynasts*, are not so
much disturbed by Zola's statement that a play is a
novel in miniature, but we are sorely tried when he insists
that a play is a scientific document. We ask for art and
Zola gives us science. And although he accuses Dumas of
preaching, he too is a preacher, not of morals but of
science, that pseudo, second-hand science which he had
borrowed from Darwin, Taine, and Bernard. Where in all
the wide world did Zola expect to find an audience that

would be cheated out of poetry and imaginative fancy? Where is the audience that will forego expressing its emotion in laughter and tears?

As is so often the case with the critic who is at the same time a creative artist, Zola's plays are not consistent with his theories. And for that very reason his dramatic works are not so impossible as one might expect after reading his dramatic philosophy. The reason for this is that he wrote his plays before he published his dramatic criticisms. We are not concerned here with his novels dramatized by Busnach and others, in which many concessions are made to satisfy a notoriety-seeking public, concessions which hurt Zola's reputation as a playwright and dramatic critic more than anything else. Of his three original plays, *Thérèse Raquin*, based on his novel, is far and away the best. It did not merit the failure which it met in 1873, for it contains elements of great tragedy. The play was written at a time when Zola, the dramatic artist, was not overwhelmed by Zola the dramatic lawgiver. It is not at all the amorphous type of play that Zola advocated in his theoretical treatises. It is extremely well-knit, and has the conventional exposition, climax, and dénouement of the well constructed play against which Zola thundered in later years; nor is it a scientific laboratory study. *Thérèse Raquin* shows here and there the hand of a dramatic genius. Its main flaw is the slowness of its tempo. The dramatist is too often superseded by the novelist, who by force of habit will stop the action to register every minute twinge of conscience.

Thérèse Raquin and her lover throw her husband into the Seine, but find no joy in their unholy love. The horror of the crime preys upon the minds of the murderers, and

their mutual recriminations, coupled with the silent im-
precations of the paralytic mother of the victim, drive the
guilty pair to suicide. The scenes in which the mother is
turned to stone on hearing the confession of the lovers and
in which her eyes accuse the tortured pair, and her fiend-
ish joy in their suffering are worthy of comparison with
scenes in Greek and Shakespearean drama. The only
other tragedy of the contemporary stage in which the
workings of remorse are represented so vividly is Tolstoy's *Power of Darkness*. *Thérèse Raquin* failed, as all
other plays of that type have failed. It is too cold, too
naked, too matter-of-fact. It inspires horror, but it fails to
inspire compassion for the victims. And, most important
of all, it lacks poetic inspiration, a quality which Zola was
more instrumental in eliminating from modern drama
than any other contemporary theorist or artist. Again, so
far as pure study of remorse goes, we have the novel in
which the author is more in his element and where he is
not circumscribed in any way. Yet *Thérèse Raquin* holds
a very important place in the drama of to-day. It became
a model for dramatists, not only in France, but in Germany, Russia, Italy, England, and the Scandinavian
countries. It was one of the war-horses of the European
theatres which sprang up in imitation of the French
Théâtre-Libre.

Les *Héritiers Rabourdin* (1874) and *Le Bouton de rose*
(1878) are unsuccessful attempts at farce. What enemy
ever prompted Zola to tempt fate with comedy? He was
totally lacking in a sense of humor and was most mala-
droit in his handling of comic situations. Inspired by Ben
Jonson's *Volpone*, *Les Héritiers Rabourdin* revolves about
a group of heirs impatiently awaiting the death of their

supposedly rich relative, who turns the tables on them by living at their expense to a penniless old age. Zola was much annoyed at the storm of hostile criticism which this play had evoked. Could not the critics see that he was reviving the cruel and cynical farce of the Middle Ages? Were they blind to the fact that he had copied Molière's turn of phrase and even bits from his plays? These whinings were, of course, meat to the critics, who pounced upon him even more ferociously. The very fact that Zola was forced to turn to the Cluny Theatre speaks volumes. The habitués of the Cluny were as capable of understanding Zola's literary farce as an American movie audience a play of Aristophanes.

In *Le Bouton de rose*, Zola once more rode to disaster, this time with an *esprit gaulois* farce, taken from one of Balzac's *Contes drolatiques*. *Le Bouton de rose* is the type of play in which Courteline might have shone; in Zola's hands the *vis comica* is conspicuously absent. As for dramatic theory, it is all thrown to the winds. *Le Bouton de rose* fairly creaks with machinery. Continued failure on the stage so irritated Zola that he lost his head. At first he accused the critics of belittling his success as a dramatist because he had already won fame as a novelist, and of begrudging him a dual power. In a cooler moment he admitted his failure as a dramatic creator, but insisted that the naturalist playwrights of the future had three models to work upon. "The public will finally listen to my plays as it finally read my novels," he prophesied; but sporadic revivals of his best play, *Thérèse Raquin*, have failed to bear out this prognostication.

Zola vowed that his personal failure as a playwright had nothing to do with the ultimate success of naturalism

on the stage. He called heaven and earth to witness that
he would continue the battle for dramatic naturalism until a genius should arise who would do for the play what
Balzac had done for the novel. He then went on writing
his dramatic criticisms, which were published during the
years 1876–1880 in the periodicals, *Le Bien Public* and *Le
Voltaire*. These were later put into book form under the
titles, *Le Naturalisme au théâtre*, *Nos Auteurs drama-
tiques*, and *Le Roman expérimental*. These books, with
the *Lettre à la jeunesse française* and the prefaces to his
plays, contain Zola's dramatic philosophy. It is unfortunate that he did not persevere in his playwriting. Even
Sarcey, one of Zola's most violent critics, admitted that,
had he not been led astray by drama-twisters like Busnach, Zola might have become a great dramatist as well as
a great novelist. Zola the dramatic failure is a far greater
artist than Zola the collaborator in sensational dramatizations.

It may seem that I have been putting the cart before
the horse by discussing Zola and his theories before the
Goncourts, Villiers de l'Isle-Adam, and Daudet, who actually preceded him on the stage. But it was Zola who
first listed the precursors of the so-called naturalist
drama; it was he who developed the theory of a new
drama and who did most of the fighting for it; and it was
he who called these precursors naturalist playwrights.
We shall see how naturalistic they were according to his
own definition of that term. In Zola's list of what I prefer
to call free dramatists, there are to my mind two errors,
one of omission and one of commission. He neglected to
mention Villiers de l'Isle-Adam's *Révolte*, and he exaggerated the value of Erckmann-Chatrian's *Ami Fritz*, a dra-

matized novel of these collaborators. *L'Ami Fritz* is a pretty idyll, entirely conventional and unoriginal. It has been one of the most popular plays in the repertory of the Comédie-Française, and owes its vogue to the fact that, appearing shortly after the Franco-Prussian War, it became a sort of sentimental call to arms. The recovery of Alsace will doubtless diminish its popularity in the years to come.

The Goncourts, Flaubert, and Daudet, Zola's fellow novelists, were all turned away from the stage either because their plays were failures or because they had difficulties with a moral or political censorship. After enjoying the flawless perfection of a work like *Madame Bovary*, it is almost a sacrilege to read Flaubert's *Candidat*. Flaubert felt as his fellow dramatists did toward the machine-made play of his day, but he had the good sense to recognize his shortcomings as a playwright, withdrew from the battle, and refused permission to have his novels dramatized. "The subject was a good one, but I botched it," he admitted. To him a play was not a novel in miniature. "The dramatic style is beginning to get on my nerves," he confessed while at work on the *Candidat*. "Those little short phrases, that continual sparkling, irritate me just like Seltzer water, which at first gives you pleasure but which soon tastes like rotten water." *Le Candidat*, a political satire, was first produced in 1874, had but four presentations, and was the only dramatic work of Flaubert that reached the footlights. Antoine tried to revive it at the Odéon in later years, but it is now completely forgotten, and rightly so.

Some years before Zola began writing plays and fulminating against contemporary drama, Edmond and

Jules de Goncourt had written their *Henriette Maréchal* and *La Patrie en danger*. The former was finished in 1863 and played for the first time at the Comédie-Française in 1865; the latter written in 1867, did not appear on the boards until Antoine produced it at the Théâtre-Libre in 1889. Neither of these plays is naturalistic in Zola's sense of the word. They are both nevertheless typical of the struggle to break away from the traditional form of play-writing, and they represent the first efforts at free drama since the work of Musset and Balzac. *La Patrie en danger* is really a historical pageant and will be discussed later with the history of the Théâtre-Libre. It is one of the freest plays of France's Free Theatre.

Henriette Maréchal is a conscious attempt on the part of the neurasthenic brothers to combine Musset's free and fanciful form with the stern realism of Balzac. As we have seen, Balzac had been a failure as a free dramatist; but when the Goncourts wrote *Henriette Maréchal*, Musset's free plays were still in process of being discovered, and some of them had not yet been produced. For instance, *Carmosine* was first played in 1865, the year of the first appearance on the stage of *Henriette Maréchal*. The Goncourt play has little of the brutal realism of the so-called naturalist plays of the latter part of the nineteenth century. In 1885, when the play was revived only to die a second death, the surviving Edmond wrote: "I do not believe in the naturalist drama, in the transferring to the temple of pasteboard conventions, the facts, events, and situations of real life." Goncourt was at that period of his life a bit piqued with Zola, who in the course of twenty years had ceased to remain the disciple that he had at first announced himself to be, and who had set himself up as the high priest of a movement which Goncourt claimed that he and his brother had originated. Indeed, Zola's *Groupe de Médan* was a sort of friendly rival of the *Grenier* of the Goncourts. Neither Edmond nor Jules fancied the word naturalism, and they were strongly opposed to Zola's rather sensational self-advertising, although they advertised themselves in what they considered a dignified and aristocratic fashion, more in keeping with the decorum of the republic of letters.

In his prefaces, or rather postfaces, to *Henriette Maréchal*, dated 1879 and 1885, Edmond was no modest violet himself in his claims to having made innovations in French dramatic form. His own criticisms are the most favorable that his play has ever received. And yet *Henriette Maréchal* has an important place in the history of the free drama of the nineteenth century. It does mark a stage in the development of dramatic theory in France between Alfred de Musset, and Becque and the Théâtre-Libre. Like Zola's *Thérèse Raquin*, to which it is much inferior, it became one of the models of the European free theatre movement, although one German critic has it that it was played in Berlin at the Freie Bühne merely because of the pretentious claims of its prefaces.

Apart from purely literary and dramatic considerations, there seems to have been a deliberately organized cabal against the play at the time of its first performance in 1865. Personal enemies of the Goncourts succeeded in driving the play from the Comédie-Française for political reasons. The Goncourts were accused by some hot-headed youths of seeking imperial favor through the good graces of Princess Mathilde. They maintained that without this help *Henriette Maréchal* would never have seen the stage, and they proceeded forthwith to kill it. The withdrawal of their play was a terrible blow to the hypersensitive brothers and the cruel Becque never tired of taunting them for their pose as martyrs to the cause of dramatic revolution. They confide to us in their *Journal* how, after fifteen years of conscientious labor, neither of them in robust health, they had pried open the doors of the Comédie-Française, only to have it slammed in their faces. They had written another *Hernani*, a revolutionary play that marked a date in the history of French drama, but an ungrateful public had destroyed two budding dramatic geniuses. Thus did the Goncourts open their hearts to an unfeeling world, which has only ridiculed them for their pretensions. Then, too, the admirers and followers of the Goncourts have hurt their cause by blindly accepting their claims. There have been two diametrically opposed groups of critics who have written on the merits of the dramatic work of the Goncourts, the one extolling them to the skies, and the other laughing at their plays and prefaces. It is only to-day that the smoke of battle is beginning to subside. We can now write more understandingly and sympathetically of the efforts of these two megalomaniacs.

Wherein lies the originality of *Henriette Maréchal?* Solely in the introduction of a masked-ball scene in the first act and in the disparity of age between the lover and his lady. The first act is in the manner of *La Patrie en danger.* It is a social pageant. The protagonists are singled out in the passing crowd and introduce themselves to us in the most stilted of expositions. The succeeding acts are pure romantic melodrama. Paul, a handsome Don Juanlet of seventeen goes to the ball in search of amorous adventure. He pays ardent court to a matron of forty, but has a rival whom he challenges to a duel. Act two finds him convalescing at the home of his unknown inamorata, Mme. Maréchal. How did he get there? He was picked up and carried there by pure chance after his duel. He becomes the accepted lover and spurns the shy advances of the daughter, Henriette. The suspicious husband attempts to surprise the lovers, but in the dark shoots the lovelorn daughter who has divined her mother's secret. Thus, in order to shield her mother, Henriette ends her own miserable existence, sacrificing her life and her honor. A little of Victor Hugo, a bit of Balzac, a goodly sprinkling of Musset, and a dash of Dumas fils in the shape of the *raisonneur* Pierre, and you have *Henriette Maréchal*. The only realistic elements of the play are those bits of notebook conversation inlaid into the plot. And yet this play was hailed as naturalist drama! It is just as romantic as *La Dame aux camélias*, a vein which the younger Dumas had outgrown. Beautifully written, poetically conceived, with a fine dramatic suspense, *Henriette Maréchal* compares favorably with the average run of play of its day, but it is in no sense epoch-making. Still the Goncourts show a far greater mastery of dialogue than Balzac, and although they failed to blend the fancifulness of Musset with the realism of Balzac, their predecessors in the free drama of the nineteenth century, their play was the first attempt since the work of Musset and Balzac to break down the tradition of the well-constructed play. Herein lies the importance of *Henriette Maréchal*.

Now for the prefaces. Edmond wrote in 1879 that he and his brother had sought to avoid the ingenious de-

vices of the modern dramatic carpenter and had tried to
introduce a bit of phantasy into the French play, a quality which even classic drama had lacked. Although they
were accused of being dramatic realists, they had no realistic theories when they wrote the play. They were desirous merely of overthrowing the old style of play and had
offered a new poetic drama in which their *langue littéraire
parlée* was an improvement upon the prose style and circus conceptions of drama of their contemporaries. He
went on to say that he was in fact a realist so far as the
novel was concerned, but found himself in total disagreement with Zola and his faithful band of followers. He admitted however that Zola was logical in his demands for a
new drama which should take the place of the romantic
play. Then comes what strongly smacks of sour grapes.
The stage was really no field for a profound study of
psychology and manners. It was suitable only for light
sketches of Parisian life in the manner of Meilhac and
Halévy. Did not Zola realize what a box of contraptions,
what a pasteboard machine, the stage really was in comparison with the fine studies that had been made through
the medium of the novel? Goncourt did not hesitate to
deny his belief in the rejuvenation of the drama, in spite
of the fact that he knew that he would be taxed as a sore-
head who had failed on the stage. The theatre in short
was sick, moribund, with its outworn dramatic conventions, its business men who had taken the place of poets,
its actresses who were but models for Worth's gowns. "In
fifty years the novel will have killed the play, which will
be replaced by trained dogs and marionettes."

Yet when the Théâtre-Libre came into existence in
1887, Edmond de Goncourt was one of its most enthusias-

tic supporters. He produced there for the first time his cherished *Patrie en danger* which had slept in a drawer for twenty-two years, wrote a one-act play for this theatre, and had three novels dramatized for it. In 1885 he had already softened his previous statements somewhat, and acknowledged that the drama was not yet dead. It could be saved only by the transfusion of two elements; first, a literary spoken language, with a poetic and lyrical note, the *summum bonum* of dramatic art, a new language in which there would be no more bookish phrases or display of authors' wit, in which the public would feel that a man of letters had forged the words of the characters. Secondly, there would have to be an expression of sentiment on the part of the characters which should be in accordance with nature, if the drama was to survive. He then nullifies this criticism, which is an excellent analysis of Musset's style, by adding, "And these rejuvenating elements I find, to be sure in an embryonic state, in *Henriette Maréchal*. Truth, there is truth in our play, more truth than one would think."

Egotistic, exaggerated, far-fetched, the critical pronouncements of the Goncourts may have been, but they were artists to their finger-tips, pathological artists to be sure, but artists with high ideals. They tried to wed art and "truth," and failed, just as Zola tried unsuccessfully to weld together science and "truth." And in their dramatic theories they included one element which Zola completely ignored — poetry. They failed to continue the new manner begun by Alfred de Musset; but their failure was not without its influence on the European drama of the nineteenth century.

Zola and the Goncourts were always looked upon during their lives as literary upstarts by the larger part of their contemporaries; they were never unanimously accepted as literary men of the first rank. But Villiers de l'Isle-Adam, whose *Révolte* is the finest example of free drama between the plays of Musset and those of Becque, was a veritable pariah. Poet, novelist, and dramatist, he is not only unknown to the general public in France, but his name does not even appear in the well-known manuals of French literature. And, what is more surprising, Zola does not mention him among his chosen few "naturalist" dramatists. This neglect is due to the fact that Villiers de l'Isle-Adam's fantastic and bizarre imagination is incomprehensible to the average French mind. He offers a close parallel in both life and work to our Poe. But then Poe is better known in France than in the United States. It seems that the French will accept literary aberrations in foreigners, but will not tolerate them from their own writers. Villiers de l'Isle-Adam is just beginning to come into his own in France, and will be known some day in this country through his *Eve future*, a satire on modern science, in which Edison assumes the rôle of a contemporary Faust.

La Révolte was first played in 1870 at the Vaudeville, and is important in the history, not only of French drama, but of European drama as well. Nine years before the Nora of Ibsen's *Doll's House*, we have Villiers de l'Isle-Adam's Elisabeth. *La Révolte* is a long one-act play entirely different from anything else the author ever wrote. It stands out just as isolated from the rest of his work as the *Plaideurs* of Racine. In it there is no symbolism, no mysticism, no esotericism. It is a straightforward, clear-cut little diamond, a satire on the materialism of to-day,

written in most exquisite French. After the fifth performance it was censored because it was considered dangerous
to public morals! A mother, a dreamer of the poetic
and the beautiful, finding it impossible to breathe longer
the same atmosphere as her materialist and selfish husband, leaves him and her child. Unlike Nora, she returns,
unable to carry out her long-conceived plan. In one act,
with only two characters, it is a masterpiece of dramatic
simplicity. Villiers de l'Isle-Adam had no pretensions to
throw overboard all conventions of playwriting. *La Révolte* has its monologues and its silences; it has long
speeches, but it possesses what most of its contemporaries
lack — poetic imagination.

In a modest preface the author disclaims any hidden
social significance in *La Révolte*. The greatest difficulty he
encountered was that he and the dramatic critics spoke
an entirely different tongue. He looked upon the drama
as an art and wrote for it as an artist, without considering
the commercial stage, just as Musset composed his *Spectacle dans un fauteuil* for readers by the fireside. And he
had a goodly array of fellow artists to support him, in
spite of the general hostile criticism which his play
evoked. Wagner, Banville, Gautier, Liszt, Leconte de
Lisle, Mendès, Anatole France, and, let it be said to his
credit, Dumas, "without whose forceful intervention this
play would never have seen the light." Antoine resuscitated *La Révolte* at the Théâtre Antoine, and to-day the
Comédie-Française and Dullin's Atelier are in dispute
over the producing rights. Several years in anticipation of
Zola, Villiers de l'Isle-Adam in his preface deplored the
stereotyped drama of his day, which "was the oppro-
brium of modern art, held in chains which dishonor

French literature. A few more dramatic adventures like this one and the Crowd will make up its mind and think for itself. . . . It will soon shrug its vast shoulders, and it will become more difficult then to paralyze materially every noble and lofty attempt of those who in all times have been creators of Art and not its valets. Justice will be done. And we have time to wait." Fifty years have passed, and critics of the advance guard are beginning to accept *La Révolte* as a far more artistic creation than most of the better-known plays of its day.

Henriette Maréchal of 1865, *La Révolte* of 1870, Daudet's *Arlésienne* of 1872, *Thérèse Raquin* of 1873, are guide-posts on the path of revolt opened up by Musset and Balzac. These four plays have all been styled "naturalist." In reality, the only one that in any way approximates Zola's term is his own *Thérèse Raquin*, which is at the same time the least free in construction of them all. Daudet's *Arlésienne* is the least "naturalist" of this group. In manuals of literature Daudet is almost universally characterized as a naturalist, but his bubbling humor, his tender pathos, his winning charm have won for him a place apart. To be sure, he did write ultra-realistic novels, but where is the "naturalism" in the immortal *Tartarin* or in the *Lettres de mon moulin?* Daudet was not primarily a dramatist. In fact, he was always unsuccessful on the stage during his lifetime; but his *Arlésienne*, his first and best play, is an extremely poetic and original achievement. Why did it fail so disastrously in 1872? There is indeed no accounting for the whims of a fickle public. It is now one of the most popular plays on the repertory of the Odéon, and Bizet's incidental music, which contains some of his finest compositions, has further helped its fortunes and makes it stand out as a unique music-drama. *L'Arlésienne* is a sentimental, tragic story of the desperate love of a Provençal youth for a worthless piece of baggage of Arles, for whom the piece is named, but who strangely never appears. Bizet's symphonies and choruses, the Provençal dances and songs, make of it a modern play illustrating better than any other in any modern language the provenance of drama which sprang originally from dance and song, a fact which modern critics too often forget. It is well that we have poetic plays of the type of *L'Arlésienne* to remind us of what the drama once was. *L'Arlésienne*, with its tableaux, its meanderings, its dances, and its music, is more of a break from the traditional play than any of its predecessors. Daudet's originality of form and poetic conception of drama completely baffled contemporary critics.

The two most potent enemies of free drama in France were Dumas and Brunetière. According to Dumas, there were only two kinds of play, the well-constructed play and the badly constructed play. This dictum illustrates exactly the point that I have been trying to make. There are really only two types of play in the latter half of the nineteenth century in France. But why call a "badly" constructed play naturalist? But to go on with Dumas. For him, the drama being an art of preparations and explanations, and the naturalists not preparing or explaining things, they are therefore not true dramatists. (As perfect a syllogism as was ever concocted.) The plays of the naturalists, being neither works of art nor mere demonstrations, are dramatic failures. As for freedom of language, the play and the book diverge widely. With the book we are two, on the stage we are three, and many a

thought that may be expressed when we are two must be
left unsaid when we are three. Aristophanes and Shakespeare would have been "more moral and more useful"
had they been more reticent in their language. A Frenchman can be pessimistic by his fireside, but French audiences want to see poetic justice done, and you must give
the public what it wants. One might just as well try to
remove all the salt from the sea as to try to modify popular tastes. Realism had reached its limits in his own plays,
and beyond that point no man might go with impunity.
Dumas summed up his theory of drama in the following
pronouncement: "The playwright who will know the human heart as did Balzac and the technique of the drama
as did Scribe will be the greatest dramatist in history."
And we have the feeling that, when he delivered himself
of that statement, he had one eye cocked on a portrait of
Alexandre Dumas fils. During his lifetime Dumas's contemporaries paid more or less attention to his plays, his
prefaces, and his moral preachings. To-morrow he will
be as dead as Scribe.

But Brunetière was the more formidable adversary.
The champion of classical traditions in latter-day France,
he was a bitter enemy of naturalism and all its works. So
ardent was he that he looked upon Zola as a personal
enemy. As for the "naturalist" drama (and even so astute
a critic as he accepted the term), he accused Zola, the
Goncourts, and Daudet of trying to write plays without
first learning the art of playwriting. He twitted them with
desiring to abolish axiomatic rules of dramatic technique
because they could not successfully employ them. He admitted that the drama of his day was suffering from a
plethora of rules, many of which might well be eliminated,

but he held firm for certain laws which he pronounced
axiomatic and fundamental. The unpardonable sin of
the naturalists was that they were guilty of confusion of
genres, which was to Brunetière a crime of literary lèse-
majesté. So unyieldingly dogmatic was he on the point of
the famous law of struggle of wills, to which he has given
his name, that he hesitated to class Musset as a great
dramatist. How could he possibly be a master of drama?
Had he not disobeyed Brunetière's law? How unfortunate
for poor Musset that he lived before the time of the new
Aristotle!

Good old Uncle Sarcey was a sort of friendly enemy of
the new movement. He tried sincerely and honestly to
understand it, but he was merciless with the scientific
theories of Zola. He was the doughty champion of the well-
made play, and died in the belief that the Dumas-Augier-
Sardou age was one of the greatest dramatic periods in
history. He wielded a tremendous influence for a generation or two in his famous column of the *Temps*, and his
verdict often meant the failure or the success of a play.
And to him a successful play was a good play. He insisted
time and again that he knew better than the playwright
when a play was a play, and declared that evolutions were
made by dramatists and not by theorists. He held that
the function of the critic was to furnish guideposts; they
should not lead the way. He was by no means the dolt
that Becque and others tried to make him out to be. He
was far more eclectic than Brunetière, and agreed for
once with Zola that Musset's plays were masterpieces of
dramatic art. In spite of the ridicule heaped upon him by
Scribophobes, he declared that as early as 1859 Scribe
had been a dead letter and that the naturalists had ex-

humed his body only to trample upon it. Furthermore, he announced Balzac's *Marâtre* as heralding a revolution in French drama. More often than not he criticized unfavorably the plays of the Théâtre-Libre, but he was a tower of strength to Antoine, who always treated him with deference. Consciously or unconsciously, Sarcey was the most conspicuous free advertising agent of the Théâtre-Libre.

CHAPTER II

HENRY BECQUE

(*And the Caravan Passes*)

"THE dog barks and the caravan passes," says Henry Becque in his *Souvenirs d'un auteur dramatique;* and all the while that Zola was vociferating manifestoes, the greatest playwright of free drama in France was struggling to get a hearing on the Paris stage. Unlike his predecessors, Becque was primarily a dramatist, yet he had few theories on play-writing, and he ridiculed both Zola and Brunetière. To him "Zola was an excellent lawmaker who wrote magnificent programmes and wretched dramatic works." And it is evidently Zola, the experimental novelist, at whom he is aiming when he says, "I have never had a great liking for assassins, hysterical and alcoholic characters, or for those martyrs of heredity and victims of evolution. Scientific criminals have never interested me." As for Brunetière's "law," he says, "No, no, there is no law and there are no rules. There are only plays, plays so different that no generalization is applicable, nor can any generalization include them all."

He finds that the plays of his generation are "abominable," but that at least they possessed one merit that the novel lacked, and that was variety. "Let us love each other just because of the diversity of our talents," he beseeches his fellow dramatists.

Let us laugh with some and weep with others. Let verse be the friend of prose and let prose give homage to verse. No preferences.

Above all, no theories. From the time of Aristotle, who had insti-
tuted, as is known, immutable rules, to that poor Scribe, whose
ridiculous maxims are still dinned into our ears, we have not been
lacking in professors of dramatic art. What have they created?
Nothing. What have they prevented? Again, nothing. . . . One single
truth seems definitive to-day; there is no measure for talent, there
are no conventions that originality cannot destroy or replace. . . .
The history of art is nothing but a struggle between original talents
and routinary minds.

Becque's own work is just as eclectic as his theories.
He wrote a libretto for an opera, a rollicking farce, a
thesis play, a romantic melodrama, comic satire, and
tragic satire. This is a remarkable record for a man who
has left behind him such a small amount of literary baggage. Between the years 1867 and 1885 he wrote only
five long plays and two one-act plays. His *Polichinelles*,
first styled *Le Monde d'argent*, which was to be his *mag-
num opus*, was left unfinished at his death in 1899, although he had begun it some fifteen years previously. His
friends invented all sorts of schemes to afford him quiet
and leisure to complete the work, but the inspiration
never came. Antoine carried him off to spend a summer
in Brittany and locked him up with his manuscript and
writing materials, but Becque's dramatic vein was exhausted. In the fourteen years that preceded his death he
wrote only five sketches, one of which is an epilogue to *La
Parisienne*. Becque explains this sterility when he writes,
"I have never had any dramatic stock to draw from. I
don't know what it is to take notes or write scenarios."
Yet in spite of this handicap, Becque has already outdistanced the brilliant and fecund trio of his day, Dumas,
Augier, and Sardou. Both his one-act plays, *La Navette*
and *Les Honnêtes Femmes*, as well as *Les Corbeaux* and *La
Parisienne*, still hold the boards.

That Becque began his dramatic career with a libretto
for an opera, *Sardanapole*, was a pure accident. Its only
importance lies in the fact that it was a determining factor in his life. It made a dramatist of a possible business
man. It shows not the slightest promise, and we must
ignore it just as Becque did himself. *L'Enfant prodigue* is
a typical vaudeville of the eighteen-sixties, gay, lively, and
witty, neither better nor worse than a thousand and one
plays of the same French genre. Sarcey having refused to
help Becque in getting *L'Enfant prodigue* produced, and
Sardou having been instrumental in assisting him, he
thereafter poured vitriol on the one and extolled the
other to the skies, albeit Sardou's idea of a play was diametrically opposed to his own.

In *Michel Pauper*, Becque begins to show his power as
a dramatist, although his play is clumsy and rhetorical.
It had been accepted by the Odéon, but its author, impa-
tient of delays, had it performed at the Porte-St. Martin
at his own expense. It is a curious mixture of brutal realism and extreme romanticism, full of melodramatic
touches. It is an abortive effort to show the power of
love and money on humanity, and has strong socialistic
leanings. "To laugh as one did at *Michel Pauper*," became a byword in Paris, and the confession of Hélène,
"He asked of his will what he could not obtain from
mine," went the rounds of the boulevards. *Michel Pauper*,
with its sudden gusts of passion, its long tirades, its violent brutality, reminds one strongly of the melodramatic
plays of Balzac. The last words of the second act, in
which the dishonest financier de la Roseraye commits
suicide, "Croak, you scoundrel," are truly Balzacian.
Hélène soliloquizes in the good old romantic style:

"Come, come, my nobleman, my warrior. . . . Come quickly, that I may admire for a moment your proud person, that I may hear your brusque and haughty voice. Bring to my prison words of liberty, songs of revolt." Michel is a superman who would conquer his place in this world and make it better, but the female monster, Hélène, drives him to madness and death.

In *L'Enlèvement* there is again a social preoccupation on the part of Becque; he would free the wronged wife from the chains of a brutal rake. The romantic and melodramatic elements of *Michel Pauper* more or less disguise the social problem, or rather problems, but *L'Enlèvement* is an out-and-out thesis play much in the manner of Dumas fils. In later years Becque expresses utter scorn for the thesis play, which is made by "patching up old bits of dramatic art, divorce, and illegitimate children. . . . I have a horror for thesis plays, which are almost always bad theses." Had *Michel Pauper* and *L'Enlèvement* been successful, Becque might have continued writing the sort of play then in vogue and would be totally ignored today. But his financial difficulties and the struggles to get his plays performed embittered him and made a misanthropist of a potential social reformer of the type of Dumas or Brieux. Failing on the stage, he had returned to business, but was unsuccessful. While waiting for the dramatic inspiration that came so slowly, he wrote for several newspapers, earning a miserable pittance. His quarrelsome nature and brutal frankness made him an impossible collaborator, and he flitted from one paper to another. In 1882 his *Corbeaux* was finally played, after being refused by playhouse after playhouse for five years, and in spite of its stormy reception, Becque suddenly found himself famous.

La Navette and *Les Honnêtes Femmes* were written in the five-year interval between the writing and the presentation of *Les Corbeaux*. *Les Honnêtes Femmes*, first played in 1880, is now on the repertory of the Comédie-Française and is the one popular play of Becque. It is a bit of worldly badinage in the manner of Musset. A young married woman repulses the advances of a bachelor friend and arranges for him a marriage with her god-daughter. *Les Honnêtes Femmes* is interesting mainly because it is entirely different from anything else that Becque has done, and it proves that he could have written plays that pleased the public, had he so desired. In *La Navette* lies the germ of *La Parisienne*. Antonia is an unmarried Clotilde who plays the game of shuttle-cock with her three lovers just as Clotilde does later with her husband and two lovers. They are the only two plays of Becque which show the slightest resemblance in theme. *La Navette* is an Aristophanesque farce with a cynical twist to it, an excellent example of modern *esprit gaulois*.

Just as Becque, in despair, was about to publish his *Corbeaux*, it was played at the Comédie-Française, in 1882, after a long and bitter controversy with the director of that house, Claretie, and with government officials. Becque was unwilling to change a single line or situation, and insisted that the play must be performed exactly as he had written it. Although it was coldly received by the public, the critics immediately stamped Becque as an original dramatist. He had at last turned the trick. He had succeeded in doing what Balzac, Flaubert, the Goncourts, and Zola had failed to do: he had written a play that was a dramatic masterpiece and yet was not in conformity with the conventions of the well-made play. He had carried out to further development the promise of free drama found in Villiers de l'Isle-Adam's *Révolte*, and had created for France a new type of play. There is nothing of Balzac nor of Musset nor of Dumas in *Les Corbeaux;* it is pure Becque. It is the study of the effects of the sudden death of a father on a family. *Les Corbeaux* are the ravens who swoop down upon a family bereft of its head. "When a man dies," says Rosalie, the faithful family servant, "and the creditors knock at the door, we can very well say, 'Here come the ravens, they leave only what they cannot carry off.'"

The first act might well have been called a prologue. The happy Vignerons are about to celebrate the betrothal of the youngest of the three daughters, when an unbidden guest, in the form of a doctor, arrives and announces the sudden death of the father. The merriment of this first act stands out in sharp contrast with the gradually increasing wretchedness of the last three acts, in which the four women are left to the mercy of the ravens, and Becque, with a refinement of cruelty, makes every man of the play a raven. That business associate, lawyer, architect, and music teacher are all ravens, we might possibly accept, but that son and son-in-law should also peck at the unhappy women seems exaggerated. Tessier, the business associate, and Bourdon, the lawyer, are the blackest of the ravens, but Tessier is caught in the mesh of his own weaving. The senile miser has taken a fancy to the plainest and most practical of the three daughters, and after being rebuffed when he proposes that Marie become his mistress, he finally offers to marry her. To free her family from want Marie sacrifices herself. The play closes with a cynical note. Tessier has just been accepted when a tradesman enters with a bill that has already been paid. "You have a man in the house now," he assures the assembled family, after summarily dismissing the last of the ravens. "Since the death of your father, my child," he says virtuously to Marie, "you have been surrounded by scoundrels."

There is very little plot to the *Corbeaux*. The first act develops a situation whose effects on the characters of the play are analyzed in the succeeding acts. Becque resorts only once to a conventional device in the first act, where he makes Madame Vigneron give a long account of the business relations between her husband and Tessier, in the bosom of her family, where these facts must have been an old story. But this is carping criticism. Throughout the last three acts the dialogue is constructed with consummate skill and each character reveals himself by his words. And the words of the ravens are cruel, sometimes needlessly cruel. They reflect Becque's black view of life. On several occasions they mar rather than help the characterization. Not all scoundrels put into words their villainous thoughts. For instance Mme. de St. Genis would most likely have broken off her son's engagement by letter instead of subjecting poor Blanche to the torture of a painful interview, calling her to her face a *fille perdue*, because she had not waited for her marriage vows. So too Merckens, the music teacher, might have dodged the obligation of helping Judith by sending her a cold note instead of bluntly telling her, "If you are respectable, you will be esteemed without being helped; if you are not, you will be helped without being esteemed."

Yet, unlike many of the *rosse* plays that were written in imitation of Becque's manner, the helpless victims of the ravens awaken our sympathies. The most beautiful sentiment of *Les Corbeaux* is the closeness with which the mother, daughters, and faithful servant cling to each other in their unequal battle with the ravens. Becque had been employed many years at the Bourse, and his experiences there had led him to believe that money was the most powerful factor in men's lives, and marriage a purely business affair. His unfinished *Polichinelles* was to have been a picture of the sordid lives of a group of financiers. Becque himself despised money and the compromises that men make in the acquisition of money. He believed himself to be a victim of the ravens of the theatres and he poured all the bitterness of his soul upon the ravens that fell upon the hapless Vigneron women.

In spite of the stormy performances of *Les Corbeaux* and the hostile notices it received at the hands of many critics, Becque was at last taken seriously as a playwright. *Les Corbeaux* shows a tremendous development in the dramatic art of Becque. Except for *La Navette*, he had given no indication of his genius. Becque states that *La Navette* was written after *Les Corbeaux*, although it was played in 1878. It is *La Parisienne* in miniature, and *La Parisienne* represents Becque's high-water mark technically. In it he carried his simplicity of plot still further than in *Les Corbeaux*, and in it he excluded all sentiment. It is one of the most impersonal plays ever written. In *La Parisienne* there is but a semblance of plot, no exposition, and no dénouement. It is one of the most perfect examples of the *tranche de vie* in modern French drama. French critics have taken exception to the title, *La Parisienne;* Becque should have generalized less and called his play *Une Parisienne*. On this point the foreigner can sympathize with

the French critic Lanson who once said, "We French have
the confounded habit of calumniating ourselves." That *la*
is merely another indication of the cruel cynicism that
Becque developed in his later years.

La Parisienne is a satire on the *ménage à trois*. Clotilde
Du Mesnil is a married woman who turns from her accepted lover to a rival, in order to procure a coveted position for her husband. Lafont, the lover, is looked upon as
a member of the household, and he and the lawful husband are made to appear ridiculous in their abject devotion to Clotilde. She has them both coming and going
with the slightest wave of a finger. Without any prelimi-
naries we are plunged from the very beginning of the play
into the heart of the situation. Clotilde and Lafont are
quarrelling over a letter and indulging in such intimate
and conjugally natural conversation, that one is immediately under the impression that they are husband and
wife. But Clotilde's admonition, "Take care, here comes
my husband," sets us aright. It is a distinct shock, and it
strikes in almost too clever a fashion the keynote of the
play. Clotilde and Lafont are lover and mistress, but they
are forever squabbling just as if they were husband and
wife. Husband and second lover are merely incidental,
and it is this parody of conjugal relations on which the
cynical humor of the play is based. Du Mesnil affects
"sublime ignorance and perfect confidence," compla-
cently accepting the comforts of home with his after-din-
ner cigar, his evening paper, and a family friend who
bears the brunt of all his wife's caprices. He sees no reason
for disturbing his peace of mind by keeping a suspicious
watch over his wife and his friend. And when lover and
lady fall out, it is the husband who mourns the absent

Lafont not so much as a friend but as a part of a comfortable household. But is Du Mesnil as asinine as he allows himself to appear, or does he wittingly close his eyes to the truth? On that point the author keeps us guessing. "Confidence, Monsieur Lafont, confidence, that's the only system that succeeds with us," says Clotilde, consoling him because he suspects his unnamed mistress. — "That has always been mine, my dear," says Du Mesnil as the curtain falls in the last act. And our final impression is that the author is winking at us behind the scenes.

The lover Lafont is a parody of the *genus homo* so frequently found in modern French drama. He is the polished, well-groomed man of the world, who seems to have no other occupation in life than the Donjuanic pursuit of other men's wives. Whether he is a complacent cuckold or a naïve victim of misplaced confidence, Du Mesnil is blissfully happy; it is Lafont who is wretchedly unhappy, consumed with jealousy and suspicion. Throughout the play, Lafont, although suspecting Clotilde's amours, is never able to place his finger on a rival. Clotilde is too wily for that. One of the most ludicrous phases of their relations is Lafont's constant preaching of respectability. Cæsar's mistress must be above suspicion. "Don't associate with that woman. Don't have anything to do with that man." He outhusbands the most husbandlike husband. He is a consummate bore, constantly catechizing and questioning Clotilde. "Where have you been?" "Where are you going?" "Who wrote you that letter?" Clotilde never satisfies his curiosity, but treats him like a puppy, and he is eternally coming back whimpering and begging forgiveness for his unwarranted suspicions.

If the men are parodies, Clotilde is not. She is the modern, perverted society woman, who has nothing serious to keep her occupied. She is frivolous, extravagant, and full of expedients. She has more charm than Flaubert's Emma Bovary. There is nothing of the animal in her. She sins because she is bored by the humdrum occupations of the housewife. She is the acme of feminine finesse and is as finished a product as is the work in which she figures. Clotilde is coldly and deliberately calculating, she is full of worldly wisdom and is a social climber. Although she is unfaithful to her husband, she is extremely solicitous about his personal comforts and his professional success. She is deeply concerned with covering up her tracks, and is most anxious about preserving all the earmarks of respectability. She is a product of our ultra-civilized world, a neurotic, constantly in search of new titillations. Clotilde Du Mesnil is one of the most superbly portrayed characters in contemporary French literature.

Yet she is not a monster. In spite of her immorality, she has moments of remorse. When she is parting from her second lover, Simpson, again a parody, this time of the sporting man who collects mistresses as one collects butterflies, she sheds a real tear. "Why do you weep?" he asks her. "Do I know?" she replies. "There is a little of everything in the tears of a woman. We are weak, fickle, and wicked, I admit. . . . The wisest thing for us to do would be to close our eyes, stop our ears, and say to ourselves courageously, 'Your place is right here, stay here.' Life wouldn't be so amusing or so palpitating, perhaps, but we should avoid many torments, many disillusions, and many regrets." Dumas would have depicted this adulteress as a vile creature, and his mouthpiece would have dissected her character, instead of allowing her to lay her own heart bare. And so Dumas will be remembered chiefly as a moralist and a reformer, whereas Becque will live as a playwright. *La Parisienne* is the *Don Quixote* of the triangle play.

Veuve! is a short one-act sketch which might be used as an epilogue to *La Parisienne*. It is even more cynical than the longer play, and is representative of the type of *saynète* which Becque wrote during the last fourteen years of his life, waiting in vain for the inspiration to finish *Les Polichinelles*. Du Mesnil has just died, the funeral has not yet taken place. Clotilde receives Lafont, but as ever there is a shadow between them. A wreath comes from Simpson and almost provokes a quarrel between the two, before the body of the husband is cold. "Did Du Mesnil suspect anything?" asks Lafont, and we can see behind the question the cruel irony of the author. "How do I know?" is the answer. "Just before he died, he said, 'You are going to find yourself in a delicate situation, with all your needs and two children to raise. You are on very good terms with Lafont. He is a man of heart and an intelligent fellow. If the thought should come to him to marry you, you must accept.'" "That's funny," says Lafont, "I thought that those things happened only in plays." Even death loses its awe in the philosophy of the embittered Becque.

Henry Becque has not yet been given due credit for the part he played in the evolution of contemporary French drama. In spite of his slight output, four of his plays are still living. *La Parisienne* and *Les Honnêtes Femmes* are on the repertory of the Comédie-Française, and *Les Corbeaux* is soon to be added. *La Navette* is, or was until recently, on the repertory of the Vieux Colombier. Thus the two most distinguished Paris theatres have recognized Becque's merits. But notwithstanding the efforts of such an artist as Réjane and the enthusiastic propaganda of Antoine, Becque has never been and never will be a popular dramatist. Critics have not disputed his ability as a dramatic artist; they have taken exception to his cynical, gloomy view of life. "He blackened the black," as Faguet has said of him. This pessimism reflects his own struggles and disillusions. His *Querelles littéraires* and *Souvenirs d'un auteur dramatique* are vitriolic in their bitterness. To anyone who did him a wrong imaginary or real, he was merciless. In his later years he came to consider himself as a martyr, although *Les Corbeaux* and *La Parisienne* had singled him out as a master in the opinions of unprejudiced critics. He was received and fêted everywhere, but the coldness with which his two masterpieces had been received by the theatre-going public and the paralyzation of his dramatic vein soured him. Then too he was no doubt influenced by the period of depression which followed the Franco-Prussian War, during which time he did his best work.

"A dramatist may have two ends in view," he says, "one to please the public, the other to satisfy only himself. I have chosen to satisfy myself." And having taken that stand, he suffered for it. He goes on to explain his method of writing plays by telling us that he never gave a character a speech without standing before a mirror and making the facial play and gestures that would go with the words. This careful study accounts for the naturalness of the dialogue in his best plays, which almost always gives the impression of perfect lifelikeness. "The drama," says Becque, "is the art of elimination"; and certainly

none of his contemporaries or followers have so mastered
the process of elimination as he did in *La Parisienne*,
where every unnecessary convention is dispensed with
and where there is not a superfluous word. In the construction of this play the movement flows along, giving
the impression of vibrating life, with the mechanism so
adroitly concealed that nowhere can we say, "This is exposition, this is climax, this is dénouement. It can be
readily understood that this sobriety of construction and
black cynicism might be exaggerated in the hands of less
skilful dramatists. Such was the case when Becque's manner was imitated by some of the writers of the Théâtre-
Libre.

Although Becque was quarrelsome and vindictive, and
for the most part lived the life of a hermit, there was a
generous side to his nature, which has not often been
touched upon. "There is in me a sentimental revolution-
ist," he says, "I imagine at times that some of my
troubles come from that source." He himself had suffered
so many rebuffs at the hands of theatre managers that it
was the dream of his life to see established in Paris a small
theatre that should be devoted exclusively to the presentation of plays by young and unknown playwrights. In
1882 he wrote:

For nearly fifteen years that I have been writing for the stage, and
it will soon be ten that I have been a member of the *Commission des
Auteurs*, I have fought everywhere for unknown authors. A useless
and mediocre undertaking, in which one is likely to make more enemies than to do any real service. Kindly disposed friends have advised me to drop that sort of thing and not bother my head with
common interests, but to stick to my own work. I feel that I should
reproach myself if I abandoned my fellow artists who are still struggling with difficulties from which I myself have scarcely escaped. I
must plead their cause. I should be very happy if their talent should

prove me to be in the right and should triumph over so much ill will. Others will come after us who ought to be happier than we, who cannot be condemned in advance to discouragement, sadness, and sterility. If there is to be a renaissance of dramatic art, it will certainly not come from the dead and from the dying. Let us encourage production as much as we can. Let us insist constantly for an outlet and support for this production. Let us demand from our theatre directors more decision and more ability. Let us insist that they be men of artistic imagination rather than men with business preoccupations.

Becque then proceeded to draw up a series of twelve articles for the guidance of the municipal officials of the city of Paris, should they be minded to do for the drama what they had done for music by way of public concerts. In them lies the germ of the Théâtre-Libre which came five years later. I reproduce them here in full:

1. There shall be created a theatre extraordinary for the making and remaking of dramatic authors.

2. This theatre will be situated in the centre of Paris. In construction, name, make-up of the company, etc., it will resemble the other theatres. Everything that might cause it to be maligned by the public will be carefully avoided.

3. A competition will be held for the position of director. People out of employment or who have failed in other walks of life must, when presenting themselves as candidates, give proof of one indispensable quality: austerity.

4. The director will perform his duties without pay, but will receive a fixed amount for each new play.

5. If, during a crisis in his management, the director should be forced to make the following decision, "Entrance to the theatre is forbidden to all those not connected with the personnel," authors can not possibly be included in that category.

6. Every play produced at this theatre shall run for three weeks, giving just enough time to prepare another one.

7. The revival of an ancient or modern play is rigorously prohibited.

8. The gratuity known by the name of curtain-raiser is suppressed.

9. The properties of the theatre should not contain more than four settings: a temple, a forest, a street, and a drawing-room. In

case a fifth setting should seem necessary by way of exception, the matter will be referred to the *Commission Supérieure des Théâtres*, which has never met since its establishment.

10. In questions concerning gowns to be paid for by the theatre, the director will make a difference between actresses who live with their families and those who live in a hotel. This distinction should favor the first category and not the second, as the director might possibly think.

11. A government official will be attached to the theatre with new duties: he will undertake to defend authors against the directors, which is contrary to the procedure heretofore in practice.

12. There will be introduced in his contract a special clause in accordance with which the director will be held to fulfill all the other clauses.

Behind the irony and personal animosity against directors that lurk within the rules for this *Théâtre de Thélème*, there stand out Becque's high artistic ideals. In certain ways he was as much of a reformer as Zola, and in spite of his scorn for Zola, Becque owes a great deal to him. Except that he was not in sympathy with Zola's scientific delusion, Becque's dramatic reforms, in playwriting as well as in producing, agree with those of Zola. One was primarily a dramatic theorist, the other a dramatic artist, yet both were reformers. *Thérèse Raquin* and *Les Corbeaux* became classics of the new drama both in and out of France.

Without the influence of these two men the Théâtre-Libre would never have been created. Antoine recognized this fact and acknowledged his debt to both. And when the Théâtre-Libre came into existence, Zola and Becque welcomed it and gave it their support.

CHAPTER III

ANDRE ANTOINE

SATAN furnished this commonplace world of ours with
its first great rebel, and every age since then has
given us its rebels more or less great. Most of the rebels
belong to the class of less great, because, once seated on
the comfortable thrones of the gods whom they have displaced, they have ceased to rebel and have joined hands
with the rebel hunters. One of the most consistent rebels
of modern times is André Antoine, founder of the Théâtre-Libre, father of the theatre that still bears his name,
one-time director of the French national theatre, the
Odéon, and to-day free-lance critic and god of the Paris
stage. And in things dramatic, Paris is France. As a pun-
ishment for his audacity, Antoine was hurled from the
heaven of the drama, but he has wrested from the gods of
convention the sovereignty of the stage and reigns to-day
supreme, yet still a rebel.

"Should you not have liked to round out your career as
director of the Comédie-Française?" he was asked recently. "Why should I want to stoop to so subordinate a
position?" was the retort. "There my hands would be
tied by sacrosanct traditions. I should be tormented by
the bickerings and squabblings of those undisciplined and
spoiled stars, the *sociétaires* of the Comédie-Française,
and I should find myself hampered at every turn by political underlings. No, I prefer to be a free-lance, for with
my lance free I wield greater power. A Cécile Sorel can

tweak the nose of the director of France's first theatre, but she cannot get back at me when I hurl thunderbolts at her for misbehaving."

Antoine did not add that his position was far more exalted than that of the present incumbent, Fabre, who presented his first play at the Théâtre-Libre, and who was a member of a group of dramatic enthusiasts that organized a similar movement in Marseilles.

There is scarcely a director, or actor, or playwright of the first order in Paris to-day who does not admit ungrudgingly his debt to Antoine. The most conservative as well as the most revolutionary acknowledge his supremacy. Without a single dissenting voice they will tell you that Antoine has raised the profession of directors (they do not call them managers in French) to the highest point that it has ever reached in France. Not only is the influence of Antoine felt in that stronghold of convention, the Comédie-Française, it has also permeated the Odéon. For several years administered by Antoine himself, that theatre is now directed by Firmin Gémier, for a long time Antoine's right-hand man at the Théâtre-Libre and his successor at the Théâtre Antoine. Lugné-Poe, Darzens, and Dullin, directors all, are products of Antoine. He has profoundly affected the lives of all those who have come in contact with him, and he is the scourge of incompetents and dramatic exploiters. His special *bêtes noires* are a group of conservative professors of the Sorbonne who still refuse to acknowledge his dramatic gods, Zola and Becque, *personae non gratissimae* in those academic halls. He was not surprised when told that Zola's name did not appear in the catalogue of the library of that institution. "They treat Zola at the Sorbonne just as the Academy treated Molière. Some day they will catch up with the literary battles that were fought and won a couple of generations ago," was his comment.

The three greatest dramatists of the Théâtre-Libre, Curel, Porto-Riche and Brieux, are all members of the Academy, Antoine having won out recently in his long-fought battle in favor of Porto-Riche. They are all still loyal friends of Antoine and are unstinting in their gratitude to him. Even Sacha Guitry, the spoiled child of the Paris boulevards, playwright, actor, and producer, pays tribute to this man with whom one would suppose he had little in common. But, then, Antoine discovered Sacha Guitry. Yet the most generous, the most whole-hearted praise that Antoine has ever received came from an entirely different camp. Most histories of French literature dogmatically state that with the coming of *Cyrano de Bergerac*, the death-knell of the Théâtre-Libre movement was sounded. The romantic poetry of Rostand had destroyed the prestige of Antoine. And yet at a gala performance held at the Opéra in honor of Antoine shortly after his resignation from the directorship of the Odéon, it was Rostand who was delegated to give the only address of the evening. After a most exquisite eulogy, the poet concluded with a sonnet:

"The stage?" You once said to me as we sat by the fireside;
"The work of a fool in the dust. . . . Hopes . . . Disgust. . . .
What poverty of means! One shouts . . . one rages . . . one's heart
    burns . . .
No, *that's not it!* . . . that is but cardboard and plaster!
And then a gentle wind passes . . . and lo, a patch of blue sky
Where for a single moment, suddenly, *That's it!*
And it's that, — that moment which consoles one for everything, —
"That," you said to me, Antoine, "is the stage!"
Life too is like that, dear friend. 'T is but for

Two or three moments of victory or of love
That the Hero pursues his task without end.
So be it! You will resume it to-morrow, tenacious spirit!
But one of those moments which makes life worth living,
Paris has given you, I think this evening!

Antoine lives in the centre of old Paris. From his
windows he looks upon the Louvre, the Seine, the old
Pont-Neuf, where once Tabarin amused the crowds. His
dining-room, which he uses as a study, is his *sanctum sanc-
torum*. Here I was confronted one day with a portly figure
of medium height, awkward in manner, dressed in pyja-
mas, in spite of the advanced hour of the day. Now I have
met celebrities in smoking-jacket and in slippers, in dress-
ing-gown and in shirt sleeves, but this was the first time
that I had met one in such intimate garb outside of a
sleeping-car. I did see Antoine in mufti once at a banquet
which he had organized in honor of Porto-Riche's election
to the Academy, and it was something of a shock. In stiff
collar and "boiled shirt," Antoine's awkwardness is ac-
centuated; in them he looks like any commonplace human
being, and the illusion of the unconventional Antoine is
destroyed. His whole life has been a battle against the
conventional, against the conventional play, conventional acting, conventional stage-setting, and conventional dramatic criticism. Antoine gives the impression of
a man of dynamic force. He radiates energy and enthusiasm and he is lacking in all the graces. That is why his
path has been so thorny in a land where the graces have
always been held in high esteem. That is why he is so
underestimated at the Sorbonne. He lacks elegance and
polish in his public utterances and in his writings. He
represents the very antipodes of academic procedure.

He belongs to the species of autodidactic men so rarely found in the United States.

I had heard that Antoine was a difficult man to approach, and so I went to him prepared to state my wants in the most eloquent French at my command. He cut off my flow of oratory at the very first phrase.

"What? You are preparing a study of the Théâtre-Libre? You are the man I have been seeking for years. The Théâtre-Libre has never been adequately treated. Come into my study. Here are forty volumes of clippings on the Théâtre-Libre. This shall be your workshop. You will find me at your elbow when you need me to fill in the gaps."

And there he left me, my speech sticking in my throat, and went back to his desk; for, despite his advanced years, he is an indefatigable worker. He goes to the theatre almost every night, and spends his days writing or reading manuscripts of plays. He reads on an average one manuscript a day, since many playwrights, experienced and inexperienced, old as well as young, submit their work to him before offering it to a theatre.

But it was not from the voluminous tomes of clippings that I received my main inspiration for writing the history of the Théâtre-Libre; it was from Antoine himself. He would come in from his adjoining workshop and would talk for hours, paying no heed to repeated calls to dinner. Only a word was needed to start him off on his reminiscences. Occasionally a name might slip his mind, but never a detail. The events of thirty-five years ago seemed as fresh in his mind as if they had happened the day before. His critical judgments were often iconoclastic, never conventional, just like the man himself, couched in most piquant and picturesque language. He never minced words in condemning those who he felt deserved censure, no matter how secure their reputation, nor did he hesitate to praise highly those with whom the majority of critics have been most harsh.

He was at his best when he talked of those men whose influence had been most potent upon his own development. When he spoke of Taine, or Zola, or Becque, or Daudet, or the Goncourts, it was with the reverence of a disciple for his masters. For Balzac his devotion comes near being a cult. By contact with minds of this kind his own mind was formed. Antoine's culture is not the culture of pure book-learning; it is the culture derived from experience in life. It must not be inferred that, for all his modernity, Antoine is not familiar with his French classics. He knows them as thoroughly as the most erudite classicist. He learned them in his youth, not from textbooks, but from the lips of Got and Coquelin, Mounet-Sully and Sarah Bernhardt. He knew them so well that when his actors at the Odéon stumbled in their lines at rehearsals, he was able to prompt them without reference to the text.

Antoine is still as open-minded as he was in the days of the Théâtre-Libre, and encourages playwrights of promise, who are seeking a foothold on the stage. Three new batches of playwrights he has discovered, one at the Théâtre-Libre, one at the Théâtre Antoine, and one at the Odéon. He is now working on his fourth series. When he comes upon what he considers a good play, he will leave no stone unturned until he succeeds in getting that play performed. And since his dramatic *flair* is remarkable, many of the directors of Paris theatres are often willing to accept his judgment. This intuition is one of the secrets of Antoine's success. They will tell you in Paris to-day, "Go to Copeau if you want to know whether or not your play is literature, but go to Antoine to find out if it is drama." Says Janvier, one of Antoine's troupe at the Théâtre-Libre, "Antoine is endowed with a marvellous intuition. In him reflection is useless. In the presence of a question to be solved, he immediately finds the natural solution, whether it concerns a gesture to be made, an intonation to be expressed, or a play to be performed." Whence it arose that Antoine sometimes let his enthusiasms carry him off his feet. His friends as well as his enemies admit that "il s'emballe."

Despite what has been said to the contrary, Antoine created no school of drama and belongs to no school. He is interested in philosophical and poetic plays provided they are plays and not mere literature. He is the least chauvinistic of Frenchman, and is the first to admit that Hauptmann is the greatest living dramatist, just as Stanislavski is the greatest producer. He has done more to introduce fresh elements into modern French drama than any man living. He belongs to an association which assists young dramatists, and is its guiding spirit. Recently an anonymous Mæcenas wished to help a struggling director who shall be nameless, and it was Antoine who was entrusted with the pleasant rôle of fairy.

He is most severe with the commercialized stage and the superficially clever fellows who write for it. There is not the slightest trace of the business instinct in Antoine. He never produced a play because he thought that it would be a financial success, nor did he ever stint money for a play which he knew would never be popular. So negligent has he been in money matters that he is in debt to-day several hundred thousand francs (pre-war francs). Antoine is the most glorious financial failure of the contemporary stage. His debts do not weigh heavily upon him. He knows, and his creditors know, that he can never pay them, but he is perfectly content with his lot, and he has no regrets for the past. He is constantly on the watch for new ideas and new forms in dramatic expression, be they French or foreign, and his enthusiasm is as fresh as when he first began to produce plays at the Théâtre-Libre.

There is something Rabelaisian about Antoine, with his ungainly figure, his unconventional presence, his unceasing labors, his scorn for worldly goods, and his fondness for good food and good wine, once his work is done. He is a diamond in the rough, and reminds one of his friend Clémenceau. The story goes that in one of his terms of office before the war, Clémenceau bade his Minister of Public Instruction install Antoine as director of the Odéon, and after hearing all the latter's faults enumerated, he remarked, "I accept him with all his consequences." And there were consequences, 750,000 francs worth of them, for according to the French system of subsidized theatres, Antoine was held personally responsible for financial losses. But when he faced his creditors, so great an impression did the sincerity of his deep love for dramatic art make upon them, that seventy-nine out of the eighty agreed not to prosecute him. The one inexorable creditor was a soulless corporation, a department store.

The men of my age [says René Benjamin] as well as their elders, have no harsher critic, nor truer, nor more inspired counsellor than

Antoine. They all feel that way, but the vanity of some of them makes them baulk at admitting it, and rather than acknowledge their weak points, they say that Antoine "exaggerates." Good heavens! How could you expect him to have the words and gestures of any ordinary person? Antoine is a storm thundering on the stage. Timorous souls beware! For thirty years he has been attacking and threatening, filled with passions. He breaks down all barriers, wins victories, and passes on, and after him the heavens open fresher and clearer. . . . This poor humanity of ours is not rich in original types. Most men belong to a species that can be recognized at a glance. Social life has cast a blight upon good old Mother Nature; she now produces things only in mass. And so what luck, when one meets, as in a story book, a figure that stands out, imposes itself, and says, "This is me, it is only *my* name that can designate *me!*" That is the destiny of Antoine.

André Antoine was a young man of about thirty when he launched his Théâtre-Libre in 1887, not too young to be without mature judgment and not old enough to have prejudices. He was born in Limoges, but he has lived most of his life in Paris. It was in large measure due to his auto-didactic training that Antoine was able to face his career of theatrical manager with an open mind. Too often the solid but fixed classical training of *lycée* and university in France destroys originality of criticism and artistic pro-duction. Antoine was the oldest of four children, and after the ravages of the siege of Paris, was sent to work at the age of twelve. He tells of his devouring as an errand boy the writings of Dumas père, George Sand, and Eugène Sue. "What a decisive influence those cheap editions had on popular education!" he wrote in later years. His avidity for reading was increased by a change of employ-ment. As a clerk for a firm of booksellers in the Paris quarter of booksellers, his higher education began. With a romantic companion who was passionately fond of litera-ture and art as his instructor, he became acquainted with the literary movement of the eighteen-sixties and seventies. At the École des Beaux Arts which was situated very near his employers, his artistic training was developed, for he found there not only examples of ancient and classic art, but also the works of the much-discussed impressionists. A chance visit to one of Taine's courses on the history of art led him to finish the series of lectures and made him an ardent admirer of the ideas of that critic, then so much in vogue. On the day of Taine's death he wrote, "He is one of the men to whom I owe most."

At other museums and libraries, especially at Sainte-Geneviève, one of the rare public institutions open in the evening, he completed his education. "My brain," he says in his *Souvenirs*, "somewhat put in order, began to classify this kind of culture which many boys of my age had not got in their schools." Thus in the haphazard self-education of Antoine, the study of contemporary art and letters came first, and made a deeper impression on his mind than the culture of the past. This accounts for his acceptance later of what was new, untraditional, and foreign.

His impressions of the theatre date from early childhood. He tells of being taken by his mother to see fairy spectacles and melodramas at the popular theatres, where for fifteen centimes one had the right to a seat and refreshments. Later, as errand boy and clerk, he divided his savings between the theatre and books. The famous actors and actresses of his day introduced him to classic and modern French plays. In 1875 he became a member of the *claque* of the Comédie-Française, thus earning extra sous to see more plays at other theatres. And what a proud lad he was when on occasion he was entrusted with the leadership of the official applauders! But he was not satisfied with seeing his idolized actors at a distance; he wanted to observe them more closely, and so he became a supernumerary at the Comédie-Française. "For a number of years I took part in the whole repertory, eyes wide-open, ears cocked for everything that happened in the great house, and I stuck as close to the actors as their shadows."

About this time he joined an evening class at a school of recitation and diction which bore the proud name of *Gymnase de la Parole*, where he made the acquaintance of Wisteaux, the future Mévisto of the Théâtre-Libre. Antoine became one of the pillars of this institution, and suggested to its director, Marius Laisné, that the pupils produce entire plays, instead of detached scenes, at their public recitals. Given a free hand, he began here his career as a theatrical manager by presenting classical plays, and won his first laurels as an actor playing the part of David Sichel in Erckmann-Chatrian's *Ami Fritz*.

In 1876, he presented himself at the *Conservatoire*, where "then as to-day it is chimerical to hope to cross the threshold without a private recommendation." He recited a well-known rôle of Got from *La Joie fait peur*. He had heard Got play this part some sixty times and aped him so closely that one of the judges exclaimed, "Il imite Got." After his examination he tried to have a word with Got, who happened to be one of the inquisitioners, but could not muster up enough courage to approach until his idol had gone several blocks. When he was told that there was no hope for him, he then and there gave up his dream of becoming an actor.

Five years of military service followed this episode. It

was as an army officer that he acquired the brusque, authoritative ways which made so many actors, playwrights, and reporters quail. On his return to Paris in 1883, he became once more a clerk in the *Compagnie Parisienne de Gaz*. In the light of these facts, which Antoine himself narrates in his *Souvenirs*, it is absurd to look upon the future actor-manager as a miracle who suddenly stepped out of a gas company and startled the dramatic world. Antoine's histrionic training was unacademic but solid.

It was not until three years after his return to the gas company that a chance invitation to witness an amateur theatrical performance reawakened the ambitious dreams of Antoine's youth. He soon became one of the most active members of the *Cercle Gaulois*, one of the many amateur dramatic clubs of Montmartre, which gave plays once a month. Not finding the repertory of popular, sentimental plays to his liking, he proposed more modern works of George Sand, Dumas fils, and Banville. But the *Cercle Gaulois* was composed of modest working folk who had never hoped to compete with a more ambitious rival, the *Cercle Pigalle*, which presented once a year an original review that attracted the attention of the great Sarcey. This superiority did not frighten Antoine, it fired his imagination. "If we amused ourselves by acting plays, there were undoubtedly other young people who spent their leisure moments writing plays." It was simply a question of finding them and combining forces. In the search for these young playwrights, Antoine stumbled into the creation of a theatre that was to revolutionize the dramatic art of France.

CHAPTER IV

THE BEGINNINGS OF THE THEATRE–LIBRE

IT WAS one Arthur Byl, who had been a member of a troupe of barnstormers and who was just blossoming into authorship, who slipped the magic idea of producing original plays into Antoine's receptive ear. He had been struck by the professional quality of Antoine's acting, urged him not to limit his talents to known plays, and magnanimously offered him a one-act play of his own composition. Thus the ball was started rolling. Byl introduced Antoine to his friend Jules Vidal, who had just published a book, and Vidal in turn not only promised Antoine a play, but put him in touch with Paul Alexis, a friend of Zola, and one of the five of the *Soirées de Médan* group. Alexis also had a play ready, and fairly took Antoine's breath away by getting a fourth play from Léon Hennique, another member of Zola's quintet. This play proved to be a dramatization of one of Zola's stories which had been refused by the Odéon. Here was a complete evening's entertainment, four one-act plays, and as an added attraction, the great name of Zola on the programme. Filled with enthusiasm, Antoine immediately set to work, and Paris had a new theatre. "As for me," says Antoine, "I had not the slightest idea of becoming a professional actor or director, and I should have laughed heartily if anyone had predicted then that we were going to revolutionize dramatic art."

These plans were made in January, 1887. At the monthly performance of the *Cercle Gaulois*, Antoine took the part of Valmoreau in *Les Idées de Madame Aubray*. Alexis sang his praises most eloquently in the "funny colyum" of the *Cri du Peuple*, a popular daily which was destined to be very helpful to the new enterprise. Alexis predicted that the Comédie-Française or the Odéon would soon be seeking Antoine, and as we shall see, the young journalist was not at all the victim of youthful enthusiasms in making this prediction. The new venture was announced with a great flourish of trumpets, and all seemed to be going well, when Antoine received a crushing setback. The *Cercle Gaulois* refused to allow him either the use of its name or the resources of the society. The more conservative members, influenced by its president, a retired army officer named Krauss, were frightened by the possible consequences of Antoine's ambitious project and the notoriety that would be attached to the *Cercle* by the presence of Zola's name. The little wooden building in the Passage des Élysées des Beaux Arts, whose diminutive hall seated just three hundred and forty-three persons, has disappeared during the recent changes in old Montmartre. It was the private property of Krauss, and the club and its modest dramatic soirées were dear to his heart. Naturally he felt a little jealous of the young upstart who was introducing radical innovations there. He would not even allow the use of the theatre for rehearsals, and consented only to rent it, for one hundred francs, for the evening of the performance. This refusal knocked the ground away from Antoine's feet, but once embarked on the sea of adventure, and endowed with a will that recognized no obstacles, he determined to sail on, even if he should have to do it at his own expense. He had been doing extra copy work, and at the end of the month the vast sum of one hundred francs would be at his disposal.

A billiard room in the rear of a cabaret served for rehearsals, Antoine paying out of his own pocket for the refreshments which were stipulated by the proprietor in lieu of rental. Then came the question of a name for the embryonic enterprise. Théâtre en Liberté was first considered, a title once used by Victor Hugo; but that name carrying with it a romantic flavor, was discarded, and Byl's suggestion of Théâtre-Libre was finally adopted. Émile Paz, a youth endowed with good business acumen and rather well-known socially, was made general secretary. A subscription circular was drawn up and the Théâtre-Libre was born.

Alexis had been doing yeoman service in the *Cri du Peuple*, but more publicity was required. So Antoine went himself to the offices of the *Figaro*, whose editor, to his surprise, published his announcement and programme. All the other important papers followed suit, and the great date, March 30, was feverishly awaited by the young enthusiasts. "Impossible to have an earlier date," said Antoine, "because it will be my salary from the gas company which will permit me to pay old man Krauss his hundred francs." Properties were loaned by Antoine's mother, and after office hours, he transported them himself in a hand-cart to the theatre for the dress rehearsals, Krauss having relented at the last moment.

It was at one of these rehearsals that Antoine met Zola for the first time. He describes this meeting: "After we finished *Jacques Damour*, the master, coming up on the stage, brought by Hennique, corners me under a gas light. I am overcome with emotion while his piercing eyes scrutinize me. A look of astonishment comes over his face and he says to me rather brusquely, 'Who in the world are you?' I stammer. He lets me flounder under his penetrating eye, and adds, 'It's very good, it's very fine! Isn't it, Hennique, is n't it very good? We'll come again to-morrow.' " To the dress rehearsal, Zola brought a group of authors and critics, among them Daudet, who was very sympathetic and cordial. As they were leaving the theatre, Daudet said, "Antoine, I see ghosts to-night in your street. Yonder is the house where I met that fiend of a woman out of whom I made Sapho." Henceforth, in triumph and in failure, Zola and Daudet heartily supported the Théâtre-Libre and, consciously or unconsciously, their sponsorship and that of Goncourt influenced to a great extent its destinies.

At last the red-letter night arrived. The performance began disastrously. Henry Burguet, having mislaid the manuscript of the introductory poem that he was to recite, lost his nerve on seeing the prompter's box empty, stumbled through the first few lines, and withdrew. Meanwhile Antoine noticed that a chair was lacking for the second play. Fortunately he had no part in the first, so he rushed out in his make-up to the nearest second-hand dealer, hired a chair, and returned with it on his head in time to save the situation. Alexis's *Mademoiselle Pomme* and Vidal's *Cocarde* left the audience cold; *Un Prefet*, Byl's contribution, was hissed; but *Jacques Damour*, the only really good play of the group, saved the evening, which, having begun so inauspiciously, ended in a burst of glory. *Jacques Damour*, Hennique's dramatization of Zola's tale, is a sort of realistic *Enoch Arden*. Jacques is a communard and refugee who has long been thought dead. Returning home unexpectedly, he finds his wife remarried. At first he fiercely demands his rights, but is finally urged to go away. All ends happily with an invitation of the second husband to stay to dinner. The weak points are the sudden change in the truculent Jacques and the cynical touch at the end which mars the beauty of an intensely tragic situation. Although only a few critics were present, the press was very favorable to the amateur players, and Fouquier gave the performance two columns on the front page of the *Figaro*. Antoine's acting was immediately singled out, one critic insisting that no professional actor in Paris could have played better the part of Jacques. Porel experienced a change of heart and asked for *Jacques Damour* for the Odéon. The Théâtre-Libre was already blazing a trail for other theatres, and Antoine once more found his destiny taking him into dramatic paths.

After the first flush of victory, Antoine, who had planned his performance as a simple distraction, saw himself at the head of a new dramatic enterprise. What was to be its purpose? Who was to support it? Requests for subscriptions had yielded little, and Antoine was personally responsible for a debt of three or four hundred francs. Nevertheless, urged on by his friends and encouraged by the many favorable newspaper criticisms, he flung discretion to the winds and began to think about a second performance of new plays.

To continue the good impression made by the first performance, the second would have to eclipse it. Byl and Vidal again offered to furnish material, but Antoine was

not satisfied with their mediocre and modest efforts. He
was for bagging bigger game, and although it was through
these two enthusiasts that he had reached Zola and his
coterie, he refused their plays. From discontent, they
passed to open hostility, but Antoine was adamant. He
thus gave the first indication of his tenacity of purpose
and unwillingness to allow personal considerations to in-
terfere with his judgment. Then too, he was looking for
a well-known author, one who would be unconnected with
the naturalist group. The press had almost unanimously
acclaimed the new venture as a naturalist theatre, and
Antoine, even at this early stage of the development of
the Théâtre-Libre, was anxious to show that he was not
in any way committed to that group. After long deliber-
ation, he picked out Émile Bergerat, the more or less
Parnassian poet, dramatist, and journalist, the *enfant terrible* of the *Figaro*, who, under the pseudonym of Caliban,
had been long protesting against the dramatic conditions
of his day. Not wishing to be beholden to anyone for an
introduction, Antoine asked for an interview with the
author, who received him "as though he were a real director," and gave him on the spot the manuscript of his
Nuit Bergamasque, which had been refused by both the
Comédie-Française and the Odéon. Bergerat brought the
younger Coquelin to one of the rehearsals of his play, and
although Antoine was grateful for his help, he found that
Coquelin "seems to attach an importance which I consider exaggerated to the preparation of what he calls
'effects.' I think that that method of interrupting the acting to wink at the public, as if to say, 'You are going to
see how funny this is,' is exactly the contrary to what I
should do."

In order to establish clearly that the Théâtre-Libre was not a public enterprise, the following invitation was drawn up:

THE THÉÂTRE-LIBRE, 37, PASSAGE DE L'ÉLYSÉE DES BEAUX ARTS

M. ÉMILE BERGERAT, M. OṢCAR MÉTÉNIER, and the charter members of the Théâtre-Libre have the honor to invite you to a performance of two dramatic experiments:

1. A realistic play in prose in one act, entitled *En Famille*.
2. A tragicomedy (in the old style), three acts in verse, entitled *La Nuit Bergamasque*.

And they hope that this double experiment, one in comic verse and the other in naturalist drama, will distract you for an hour or two from the cares of everyday-life.

Performance of May 30, 1887.

This time all literary and artistic Paris came to see what was being done by the amateurs who had made such a stir. Bergerat brought his newspaper colleagues and his friends among the Parnassians. The press was represented in full, and the leading men of letters, actors, artists, and musicians of Paris filled the tiny theatre to overflowing. Bergerat's *Nuit Bergamasque* was an attempt to revive comic drama in verse, a genre which he regretted had fallen into desuetude. Based on one of Boccaccio's tales, it has a mediæval flavor of the Italian *commedie dell'arte*. In it a young poet and an adventurer are in conflict with an old miser over the possession of the latter's mistress and slave. The play is an amusing *tour de force*, eminently fitted to please a literary audience. But Méténier's *En Famille* was a horse of a different color. It was one of the earliest of the one-act plays produced at the Théâtre-Libre, in which Paris low life is depicted. It is a *tranche de vie apache*, a sort of "penny

dreadful" in dramatic form, the kind of piece that may
still be seen at the Grand Guignol. It was taken from a
story written by Méténier himself, and its chief dramatic
interest is centered on the description of the execution of
a friend of the family. "A monologue on the guillotine,"
one of the critics called it. The author himself had his
doubts about it when he referred to it as "very daring
and violent." Sarcey, who was on the outs with Bergerat,
did not mention *La Nuit Bergamasque*. After praising the
technical qualities of the performance, he said of *En
Famille* that if that sort of thing was to be the drama of
the future, he hoped he would be gone before it arrived.

Whatever disagreement there may have been as to the
literary and dramatic values of the plays, the press was
unanimous in recognizing the high quality of the acting
and the scenic detail.

How rare it is [commented one critic] to find a director who has no
check-room for wraps, yet who has put such meticulous care and
thought into acting and setting. The dramatic muse feels at home
here, right in her element, an element that is familiar, pleasing, and
not at all modest, albeit at times a little naïve. Here everything is
natural, even the sign placed over the door inviting the last one out
to turn off the gas.

Lemaître, who followed so sympathetically the work of
the Théâtre-Libre, in spite of frequent harsh judgments,
has left a charming description of the little building
where Antoine's venture was born.

Toward half-past eight in the evening, you might have seen some
shadows gliding along the booths of the street-fair of Montmartre,
and carefully avoiding the puddles of water on the pavements of the
Place Pigalle, scrutinizing through their *lorgnettes* the nameplates at
the corners of the streets; no passage, no theatre! We finally make for
the light of a wine-shop and we enter a steep and winding alley,
dimly lighted. A line of cabs is slowly climbing up. We follow them; on

each side, shadowy buildings in ruins, and dirty walls, at the far end
an obscure flight of steps. We looked like magi in topcoats, seeking
a hidden and glorious manger. Is it the cradle where will be reborn the
drama, that decrepit and doting old man? I can't answer for that
yet. All that I know is that we passed a very amusing evening at the
Théâtre-Libre.

The hall is very small and rather naïvely decorated; it resembles
the concert hall of a county-seat. One might stretch out one's hand
to the actors over the footlights and put one's legs on the prompter's
box. The stage is so narrow that only the most elementary scenery
can be used on it, and it is so near us that scenic illusion is impossible. If there is any illusion, it is because we ourselves create it, just
as, in Shakespeare's time, the audience saw what a sign commanded
it to see, and in Molière's day, the action of a play was in no way disturbed by the goings and comings of the candle-snuffer.

The foundation of the Théâtre-Libre and the terrible
disaster of the burning of the Opéra-Comique were the
outstanding events of the Paris dramatic season of
1886–87. Antoine was from the very first taken seriously
as a producer, and he was immediately recognized as one
of the leading actors of Paris. "It is from the Gas that
we get our light to-day," said the wag, Désiré Luc.

For a long time there has been a demand for a new theatre where
dramatic experiments might be tried out with absolute independence.
But who was there daring enough to establish such an institution?
Who would foot the heavy expense of such an enterprise? A Mæcenas was looked for, and behold, a Job appeared! . . . Antoine has the
vocation of the boards and a remarkable intuition. His face, with its
prominent jaw and firm lips, indicates a tenacious will. His blue eyes
are clear and cold. All this shows how authoritative he is. As an actor
he is more natural than studied; his bearing surprises and impresses
the audience.

The Théâtre-Libre was no dramatic miracle, as so
many of Antoine's admirers have claimed. His long, self-
made preparation, his unbounded energy and determina-
tion, coupled with his disinterestedness, made his theatre

possible. This disinterestedness was shown early in the history of the Théâtre-Libre, by his refusal to exploit *En Famille* at the Chat Noir. Salis, the enterprising manager of that artistic cabaret, offered Antoine flattering inducements to produce this play there; but in spite of the temptation to raise money for his debts by this means, he realized that the appearance of the Théâtre-Libre troupe at a cabaret would hurt the literary and artistic reputation that the embryonic movement had won, and so he wisely refused this offer.

During the month of June, projects for a complete theatrical season for 1887–88 began to ferment. Catulle Mendès became an active supporter of the Théâtre-Libre and promised a play in verse. Encouraged by the backing of Bergerat and Mendès, Antoine then went to Banville, who, after hearing him recite "La Ballade des Pauvres Gens" from that poet's *Gringoire*, agreed to let him have his *Baiser*. With three poets in his camp to offset the influence of the naturalists, Antoine went ahead with his plans. Peace was made with Byl and Vidal, who had helped him so much in the beginning. They agreed to furnish an adaptation of the Goncourts' *Sœur Philomène*. Tolstoy's *Power of Darkness*, which had just appeared in a French translation, was added to the ambitious list. All these important names would lend prestige to the new theatre and would be mingled with the modest names of younger unknown playwrights.

While all these glorious plans were seething in Antoine's mind, Porel invited him to call at the Odéon. "My dear fellow," he began, "you are evidently an artist. I have seen one or two of your performances; they are very amusing, a little Bohemian, but not serious at all." (This from the man who had at first refused *Jacques Damour* and who had asked for the play after seeing it performed at the Théâtre-Libre.) "You have no illusions as to that, have you? It is a dramatic workshop for a little group of Parisians; before six months, all these people will be tired of it and will leave you. Profit by this bit of good fortune and since you dream of being an actor, seize this opportunity of getting a fine position. You have perhaps talent and a future; your temperament for the stage is real, but you don't know your profession. Come and learn it with me. At your age one is satisfied with little. I'll give you five hundred francs a month and you will make your début in a revival of Augier's *Contagion*, the chief rôle of which was created by Got. It will just suit you."

Antoine was for the moment flattered at seeing the dreams of his boyhood realized, but, fortified by the support of his friends, and with more ambitious ideas in his head, he refused the offer on the ground that he had already promised to produce certain plays the next season. He expressed the hope that he might be considered for the year following. It was, in the end, as director, and not as a simple actor, that Antoine was destined to enter the Odéon.

Antoine's original plan had been to perform the plays of young, unknown dramatists. The plays of the well-known writers were to be used merely as an added attraction to win an audience. But where were these young dramatists? He wrote to Sarcey, who published his letter in the *Temps:*

Do you know that it is no laughing matter to be a director? I am organizing for the Théâtre-Libre six or seven performances, a whole series for next season. I shall have something from Zola, Goncourt,

Catulle Mendès, etc. All the well-known men answer my appeal with great kindness; but the young men? Well, I don't see them come, although I knock at all doors, at studios, literary coteries, and cabarets. I have received nothing to date, except the work of old men and old women whose efforts reek of the provinces. They bring me things in verse, the like of which I should have never imagined. What is the reason for this? Can it be that directors are not, after all, such bad fellows as they are painted? I beg of you, Monsieur Sarcey, save the Théâtre-Libre, which is going to be a gallery of the illustrious, instead of being, as I had hoped, a refuge for the young, and a trial laboratory. Have n't you anything for me? I imagine that you must receive plays by the dozen. Send me the works and the authors, I pray you.

Sarcey, who was the *bête noire* of unsuccessful and unconventional dramatists, but who was always kindly disposed to Antoine, — although he was more often than not out of sympathy with the plays of the Théâtre-Libre, — inserted a line of his own, saying that the director of the tiny theatre was a man of great energy and intelligence, adding that, unfortunately, he, Sarcey, had nothing to send to the new theatre. A few days later, he announced that, as a result of the publication of Antoine's letter, requests for his address had come pouring in from all parts of France.

The resourceful Paz had found a printer willing to furnish on credit two thousand copies of the prospectus that had been prepared, and Antoine wrote over a thousand personal notes, fearing that a cold printed notice would not make a sufficient appeal. To save postage, he delivered circulars and letters in person! The last one had gone to its destination at dawn on the morning of the twenty-fifth of July, a memorable date for Antoine, for on that day he burned his bridges behind him and resigned from the gas company. He was fully conscious of the fact that he was committing a rash act, but he realized that subscribers could not be found while he was pushing a pen for some one else all day.

Then followed a period of deep discouragement. After nearly three weeks of waiting, there came only one subscription in reply to thirteen hundred requests. Albert Wolff of the *Figaro*, to whom Antoine had written for help just as he had done to Sarcey, threw cold water on the project by inviting Antoine to come to see him in September. But Bergerat, who was on the same paper, came to the rescue once more with a flattering article on the "Little Odéon," which brought in a marquis who, instead of the desired hundred francs, offered Antoine the libretto of a comic opera of his own composition. By the first of September, twenty-four subscribers had been found, and on the strength of their twenty-four hundred francs, a studio with an adjoining salon was hired as a business office and rehearsal room, incidentally providing a lodging for Antoine. Kind friends treated the penniless director to an occasional square meal. Young authors began to interest themselves in the new theatre, and 96 Rue Blanche became the permanent home of the Théâtre-Libre. The young poet Rodolphe Darzens, now director of the Théâtre des Arts, was made archivist of the perfected organization. All the newspapers published the programme for the season, warning their readers that Antoine's venture must be taken seriously.

CHAPTER V

THE BATTLES OF THE FIRST SEASON
(1887–1888)

WITH thirty-seven subscribers and a debt of several thousand francs, the Théâtre-Libre opened its first full season in October, 1887. The names of Goncourt and Villiers de l'Isle-Adam appeared on the first programme, a dramatization of the novelists' *Sœur Philomène*, and *L'Évasion* of the Bohemian poet. *Sœur Philomène* was looked forward to with eager anticipation and was rather favorably received. It is really only a series of dramatic tableaux taken from the novel, and it contains only one scene that can be called dramatic, that of the nun's prayer at the end. The second tableau is far the better of the two, and the sentimental attraction of the doctor for the nun Philomène is very delicately handled. *L'Évasion* is another blood and thunder one-act horror of the kind that still flourishes at the Grand Guignol. It is in no way comparable to *La Révolte* of the same author, and was saved only by the superb acting of Mévisto, who shone in *Apache* rôles. His realistic portrayal of the cut-throat Pagnol, who prefers fat bourgeois for victims, brought down the house.

Both plays caused a considerable sensation, the result of which was disastrous to Antoine. The timid Krauss did not relish the publicity which the Théâtre-Libre was bringing to his toy playhouse, and he refused to rent it any longer, on the ground that the tumultuous applause and stampings of Antoine's enthusiasts would wreck his building. After a long search, a little theatre was chosen in the Montparnasse quarter, in the Rue de la Gaîté, which was considered at that time off the theatrical map. The director of this theatre, one Hartmann, agreed to rent it on Friday evenings with all its accessories, at Antoine's own price. There was violent opposition to this Montparnassian move at the Rue Blanche and a speedy disaster was prophesied. But in spite of all fears the first performance was a huge success financially. Although the hall held only eight hundred, there were over three thousand requests for seats, the result being that there was endless confusion at the door, and several celebrities were unceremoniously handled. Catulle Mendès, who had shown a friendly interest in Antoine, and who had smoothed his path in many ways, presented his *Femme de Tabarin*, which was the hit of the evening. The following dedication to the printed version of the play is an indication of Mendès's attitude toward Antoine.

The stage where you perform plays with your young comrades is the consolation of old romanticists as well as the hope of the young naturalists. You welcome, you seek, daring, new, singular works. What is not of the theatre, you play in your theatre and the audience applauds. In a few evenings you have done for dramatic art much more than many directors have done for it in years. It is perhaps from the inauguration of your free boards that one must date the renaissance of real drama, of real comedy and of real farce. You have made only one mistake, that of asking of me *La Femme de Tabarin*. I am afraid that the brutal brevity of this burlesque and tragic scenario may disconcert the indulgence of thec ritics and the public.

Mendès's play had been published in 1874 and it is one of the early works of the poet. He called it a *tragi-parade*, and it is in fact more a Punch-and-Judy opera than anything else. Mendès adds a tragic touch to the Tabarin cycle by making the famous clown really kill his wife. *Jacques Damour* had been taken by the Odéon, *La Femme de Tabarin* was taken by the Comédie-Française. In two performances, the Théâtre-Libre had imposed its standards on the two state theatres of Paris.

Hennique's *Esther Brandès*, which was performed the same night, is one of many plays of the free dramatists of the Théâtre-Libre with little action and much analysis of character. But Esther's motive for desiring the death of her brother-in-law, on which the play hinges, is none too clear. In a novel the author might have driven home his point. Hennique, a satellite of Zola, illustrates better than Zola himself the gropings of the theorists of free drama.

The mismanagement of box-office affairs at the second performance had, however, made many enemies among the critics, and Antoine was accused of trying to make money out of the sensational plays offered at the Théâtre-Libre. The preceding year, Caran d'Ache with his famous silhouettes had been the chief Parisian attraction; this year the great sensation was the Théâtre-Libre. Antoine combated hostile criticism by strengthening his troupe, taking one actor from one theatre and borrowing another from a second. Émile Paz resigned, probably because of the storm of criticism evoked by his carelessness, and one Montégut, a nephew of Daudet, who was on the staff of *L'Intransigeant*, took his place. For the next performance Antoine decided that he must outdo himself in order to efface the bad impression made at the opening performance of the season. With the help of such famous names as Zola and Banville, he actually did overcome all opposition, and his theatre was packed for the second performance. The critics were unanimous in pronouncing it the best yet given. Banville's *Baiser* was immediately sought by the Comédie-Française, where it still forms a part of the repertory. It is a charming little fairy play in verse, a *Midsummer Night's Dream* in miniature, exquisite, dainty, and poetic. It was easily the best play of the evening, and the poet, Banville, then in advancing years, was given an ovation.

"They play like angels," said Banville to Zola. "Where in the devil did they learn to recite poetry?"

"Oh," answered Zola, "It is players like these we have long needed."

Céard's *Tout pour l'honneur*, a dramatization of Zola's *Capitaine Burle*, ran *Le Baiser* a close second. It is one of the very few of Zola's themes that does not leave a bad taste in the mouth. Céard was another member of the Médan group who beginning his playwriting career with an adaptation of the Goncourts' *Renée Mauperin*, ended by becoming a member of the Goncourt Academy. In *Tout pour l'honneur* a grandmother forces her grandson to shake hands with the man who has killed the boy's father in a duel to save the honor of their family. Lemaître was loud in his praise of the playlet, which he found in the spirit of Corneille. Sarcey saw in it nothing but the dénouement of a tragedy, the first four acts of which had been suppressed. Both were right; it was a dramatic episode *à la Corneille*.

Most critics were flattering in their verdicts on these two one-act plays. But the work which was to influence the destinies of the Théâtre-Libre, and which created the most comment, favorable as well as unfavorable, was Jean Jullien's *Sérénade*. According to Céard, it was a revolutionary piece of writing which "created at the out-set what was later called *genre Théâtre-Libre! La Sérénade* is the type of play which the French call *rosse*, and which, as Céard says, became associated generally with the Théâtre-Libre in spite of all Antoine's efforts to avoid restricting his theatre to plays of one single school. *Rosse* is a word that almost defies translation. Let the French critic, Filon, define it: "*Rosserie*," he says, "is a sort of vicious ingenuousness, the state of soul of people who never had any moral sense and who live in impurity and injustice, like a fish in water."

Jean Jullien was looked upon as the leader of a young group of free dramatists who had attached themselves to Antoine's banner. In spite of the praise lavished upon him, he did little but restate, in his *Théâtre vivant*, theories already advanced by Zola, Strindberg, and Ibsen. Although Jullien produced three plays at the Théâtre-Libre, two of which were of the *rosse* type, he rebuked Antoine some years later for producing that very kind of play. Jullien's greatest title to fame is the coinage of the phrase, *tranche de vie*. "A play is a slice of life artistically put on the boards." But there is only a small measure of originality in this statement which is merely a paraphrase of Zola's *lambeau d'existence*. It seems, however, to have captured the imagination of the younger dramatists at the Théâtre-Libre, and completely replaced Zola's phrase. Taking another cue from Zola and Strindberg, Jullien advocated abolishing the footlights, urging that in life light comes from above and not from below. Ibsen sup-plied him with the idea that the stage is a room with the fourth wall formed by the curtain, transparent to the public, but opaque to the players. He argued that the

Comédie-Française should not produce modern plays; it should be the Louvre of dramatic art, just as the Odéon should be the Luxembourg. Following Zola again, he was for sweeping away all that had gone before in the drama. For a new age, there must be a new type of play. Like Zola, he advocated the introduction into France of foreign plays, especially those of Ibsen and Tolstoy. He differed from Zola, however, in that his vision was not obfuscated by any scientific mania, and he insisted that the aim of the dramatist should be to interest the public and arouse emotions. His dramatic god was Becque, whose cynical mood he exaggerated in his early Théâtre-Libre plays.

But what emotions did Jullien expect to arouse by *La Sérénade*, that blatantly cynical and crude picture of a quadrangle? It is true, as he says, that there is incest in the Greek drama. Ah! but what horror it arouses! What terrible and bloody scenes result! How can we be expected to be moved by a play in which a mother and daughter are mistresses of a family tutor who is finally accepted as a son-in-law by a complacent father? We could far better understand the general butchery of the conventional play. We might then pity the wretched victims. Does the author expect us to laugh at the discomfiture and torture of the husband and father? *La Sérénade* is a too obvious revolt against the classic French tradition in its mingling of the comic and the tragic. But if the author does not make it clear to his audience when he means to be comic and when he means to be tragic, then he falls between two stools. *La Sérénade* is an unsuccessful endeavor to outdo Becque. Yet it is only fair to say that in later years, Jullien tempered his violent unnaturalism, but when he ceased to be extreme, he became banal.

In January, 1888, Antoine accepted an invitation from the Théâtre du Parc to play in Brussels. Only he and Marie Defresne were able to leave Paris; the other actors were furnished by the Brussels theatre. The repertory consisted of *Le Baiser*, *La Femme de Tabarin*, and *Jacques Damour*. Antoine was somewhat concerned about his appearance before his first general public because of his weak voice, but the tour proved a success artistically as well as financially. Mendès, who was well known in Brussels, and who had arranged the visit, accompanied him and presented him to the literary and artistic world of the Belgian capital. Antoine was much encouraged by the success of the venture, which netted him more in a single evening than he had been able to earn in a month at the gas company.

The studio in the Rue Blanche, which was the real home of the Théâtre-Libre, was beginning to be looked upon as an important literary and artistic centre of Paris. Loafers and dilettantes were not encouraged to lounge there; only serious workers were welcome. Many mature writers and artists to-day look back upon it as the cradle of their youthful hopes.

It was a large square salon with divans. On the walls were canvases by young realistic painters. They give the note to the establishment which has a youthful atmosphere. Antoine is the general-in-chief of this army of volunteers. He insists that everyone, like him, shall take his mission seriously. And from nine o'clock in the evening until midnight these young people manœuvre with admirable discipline, reciting dialogues or monologues with fury, until they find the right note or the true gesture, as if they were paid dearly for that, and as if they were not working for glory alone.

The next play, Tolstoy's *Power of Darkness*, had been forbidden the stage in Russia. Its presentation at the

Théâtre-Libre was without a doubt the most important theatrical event of the season. France had never been hospitable to foreign dramatists, and the *Power of Darkness* was the first of a series of foreign plays that was to make the Théâtre-Libre famous. The Théâtre de l'Œuvre, the Vieux Colombier, the Atelier, and the Comédie des Champs-Elysées, have continued that tradition started by the Théâtre-Libre, and to-day Paris is as hospitable to foreign drama as any city in the world. Dumas, Augier, and Sardou had been questioned as to the possibility of producing Tolstoy's play in Paris, and all three had advised against it. Dumas found it too sombre, its language incomprehensible to the French. Sardou found it cruelly true and beautiful, but a thing to be read, not seen. Augier considered it less a play than a novel in dialogue form. And Sarcey was proud to go on record against it with the great dramatic triumvirate. Antoine's appetite was of course whetted by this opposition of the conservatives. Was not his Théâtre-Libre a theatre of opposition? Not satisfied with an existing translation, he had another one prepared by a Russian named Pavlovsky and Oscar Méténier, the young author of *En Famille*. The private performance awakened such curiosity that a public one had to be given. The Vaudeville wanted to take it, but Antoine gave it to Hartmann, the director of the Montparnasse theatre who had been so helpful to him. In spite of a snow-storm, the theatre was filled, and for the first time the theatre-going public of Paris had an opportunity to judge the calibre of the work of the Théâtre-Libre.

The criticisms of the conservative press remind one very much of the attitude of the critics of the eighteenth century in France toward Shakespeare. To them and even to their most distinguished representative, Voltaire, Shakespeare was a barbarian of the north. So it was with Tolstoy a hundred years later. Melchior de Vogüé, who has done so much to introduce Russian literature to France, wrote a most flattering article on Antoine's performance for the *Revue des Deux Mondes*. He maintained that, although Tolstoy may not have been so finished an artist as the ancient Greek dramatists, he showed a like profundity. He asserted that it was just as false to judge Russian peasants from the characters in the *Power of Darkness* as to judge the French people in the light of naturalist literature. Tolstoy had written the play with a deep moral purpose. He wanted to show to what animal degradation drink might lead the ignorant peasant. Vogüé admitted that the *Power of Darkness* was exceedingly difficult to translate because of the mutterings and unfinished phrases. The title itself had two meanings, night and evil, the idea in Tolstoy's mind being that darkness engenders one crime which is the mother of another, just as in Greek tragedy. Vogüé waxed enthusiastic over the acting and setting of Antoine's performance, his only adverse criticism being that Antoine had not used the variant offered by Tolstoy himself for the scene in which the child born in adultery is murdered. With this variant,—now used by Pitoëff at the Comédie des Champs-Élysées, — which puts the revolting spectacle off stage, the *Power of Darkness* becomes one of the loftiest expressions of modern tragedy. Only Zola in his *Thérèse Raquin* has risen to such heights in the portrayal of the ravages of remorse. With its performance of the *Power of Darkness*, the Théâtre-Libre sprang into international fame.

The Théâtre-Libre seemed destined to remain in the limelight. The March performance was given over to a group of young authors who had drawn up an anti-Zola manifesto which had appeared in the columns of the *Figaro*, at the time of the publication of *La Terre*, and had created a mild stir in Paris. Instigated by Bonnetain of the *Figaro*, it was signed by him, by Lucien Descaves, J.-H. Rosny, Gustave Guiches, and Paul Margueritte. These writers, in search of notoriety, repudiated Zola in a long flamboyant article. The laugh was really on them, because Zola quietly ignored them, and his enemies refused to take the hot-headed youths seriously. Antoine disapproved of this puerile rodomontade on the part of his young friends, but with the consent of Zola himself, he offered them an opportunity to show what they could do on the stage. He welcomed an occasion to prove that although he had a great admiration for Zola and agreed with him on many points, he was in no way desirous of making the Théâtre-Libre a laboratory for Zola's dramatic theories. Antoine maintained, from first to last, that the Théâtre-Libre was not exclusively a naturalist theatre, and a careful examination of his programmes will dispel the current notion that he was Zola's tool. Antoine was producing plays that were refused elsewhere, and these plays were, for the most part, of the ultra-realist type.

As finally made up, the programme of the manifestants included only four of them, Lavedan's name appearing in place of Rosny's. The audience, which had expected something most un-Zolalike, in accordance with the doctrines expressed by the dissenters, was keenly disappointed by the mediocre results of their dramatic efforts. The

plays were extremely realistic in spirit, and the longest
of them, *La Pelote* of Bonnetain and Descaves, resembled
rather closely Zola's *Héritiers Rabourdin*. In *La Pelote* a
group of harpies, the family of a housekeeper to a rich
and senile old man, employ ruse and blackmail to rid
themselves of his heirs. The rest of the programme consisted of amateur sketches. "Funereal, lugubrious," was
the almost unanimous cry of the critics. Sarcey, who had
been coming regularly to the Théâtre-Libre, always re-
specting, but never understanding, Antoine's efforts,
hoped to find at last something original in these anti-
Zolaists. In the performance of the manifestants he saw
only a new effort to *épater les bourgeois*.

> They are all fine fellows [he said], but not artists. They seem to
> take pleasure in making fun of my good nature and credulity. . . . It
> is not the Montparnasse Theatre at which Antoine's company is
> playing, it is the Montparnasse Cemetery. Every month when we re-
> ceive our tickets of invitation, it seems to us that we are reading a
> notice of Antoine's funeral and we go to see him die with great
> pleasure.

But Antoine plodded along, undiscouraged by hostile
criticism and unspoiled by indiscriminate praise. He had
the joy and satisfaction of lending Mévisto to the Porte
Saint-Martin and Madame France to the Ambigu, thus
returning courtesies to the regular theatres which had
lent actors to him.

In the April performance, Antoine tried again to
counter the impression that the Théâtre-Libre was a naturalist playhouse. Both plays on the programme were in
verse. Émile Moreau's *Matapan* had been written in 1885
but had never been produced. It is a rather dull satire on
newspapers and contemporary politics. Paul Arène's
mediocre dramatization of Théodore Aubanel's Pro-

vençal poem, *Le Pain du Péché*, is based on the Provençal legend that food prepared by an adulteress and her lover will poison her children within the year. The two plays were poorly performed and failed to advance the fortunes of the Théâtre-Libre.

The first season of Antoine's theatre closed with a performance which convinced the public, in spite of all protestations, that the Théâtre-Libre was bound hand and foot to Zola's school. Alexis, Ancey, and Salandri were all closely associated with the Théâtre-Libre movement, and their plays, *La Fin de Lucie Pellegrin*, *M. Lamblin*, and *La Prose*, followed the vogue started by Jullien's *Sérénade*. "For a single kiss, what agonies!" wrote one critic who longed for more poetic works like Banville's *Baiser*. Salandri, who had already written a couple of dramatic trifles in collaboration with his former school companion, Brieux, presented his first original play, *La Prose*, at the Théâtre-Libre. It is difficult to understand in what way Salandri has contributed to modern French drama. Although his fellows of the Théâtre-Libre, dramatists as well as critics, have gone out of their way to praise him, he has always struck me as a near-dramatist. In no play of his, presented at the Théâtre-Libre or elsewhere, does he seem to have sounded a firm note. He is a wavering half-and-half realist, not quite daring enough to put the crudities of Jullien and Ancey into the mouths of his characters, and at the same time unwilling to identify himself with the more conventional playwrights. *La Prose* is naïve, puerile, hesitating realism, based on one of Salandri's own novels. The heroine, Berthe, is unwilling to accept the husband proposed by her well-to-do parents and runs off with her father's clerk. After spending a night with her sweetheart's family, she is so disgusted with the vulgar, tawdry surroundings that she returns home in a chastened mood, ready to marry a more respectable suitor. Life to Salandri is a dull, prosaic affair, and "a man is like a piece of goods which must be examined before being purchased."

The best play of the trio was Georges Ancey's *M. Lamblin*. Ancey's name, like that of Jullien, has always been associated with the *théâtre rosse*. And Ancey and Jullien were more instrumental than any other writers of the Théâtre-Libre in causing it to be identified with dramatic *rosserie*. *M. Lamblin* was the first play of this young author, who, more than any other dramatist of the Théâtre-Libre, allowed his brilliant talent to be unduly influenced by ultra-realistic language and situations. All the other playwrights, including Jullien, gradually toned down their realism with maturer years. Not so with Ancey. His plays are pure *rosserie*, and he was not heard from after the closing of the Théâtre-Libre. *M. Lamblin* is one of a series of plays by Ancey in which man the egotist is portrayed in a cynico-comic vein. Lamblin, seconded by his mother-in-law, rejoices in the fact that he can eat his cake and have it, too. He wants all the comforts of a quiet home and a virtuous, loving wife to minister to his needs, but he also insists upon having a mistress to furnish him a little excitement. Now this may not seem a very original philosophy, but Ancey has given it a burlesque touch which makes the play a model of its kind. He is, however, incapable of sustained effort, and he shines only in short sketches like *M. Lamblin* and in detached scenes of his longer plays.

Paul Alexis's *Lucie Pellegrin*, also a one-act play, involved Antoine in one of the bitterest controversies in the history of the Théâtre-Libre. *La Prose* is mild, half-baked realism, *M. Lamblin* is comic *rosserie*, but *Lucie Pellegrin* is pure pornography. It is difficult to understand why Antoine allowed himself to be stampeded into putting on this inartistic bit of photography disguised as a play. Alexis, who had already collaborated in an insignificant one-act piece produced on the opening night of the Théâtre-Libre, never was a dramatist, and *La Fin de Lucie Pellegrin* was only another of the many unsuccessful essays by novelists of the Zola school to dramatize their short stories and novels for Antoine. The action centres about a dying prostitute who, surrounded by her friends, tells anecdotes of their lives and hers. The play shows the lowest depths of degradation to which the human body can fall. The actress who took the part of a sodomitic character apologized for so doing in the press. Few of the critics hazarded to tell the plot in their columns. *Lucie Pellegrin* is entirely bereft of any artistic touch, and represents the extremes of realism, foul in language and vicious in its characters. Such a play was naturally pounced upon by the enemies of the Théâtre-Libre, who poured column after column of vitriol upon the perpetrators of such an outrage to the canons of literary good taste.

Are these youths whose plays Antoine presents [asks Sarcey], mere hot-air artists who take pleasure in mystifying their contemporaries, or are they giving us in good faith the enormities which we heard last evening? I have the highest esteem for M. Antoine. He has dramatic taste, he seems to possess all the qualities which go to make up an excellent director, and it is directors we lack rather than actors. He has rendered great service to dramatic art and will render still greater service when he frees himself from the influence of certain coteries to which I think he is fettered. We love the theatre each in his own way, we love it passionately, both of us, and there is in that love, in spite of divergence of opinions, a tie which is very strong. But I must insist very clearly to M. Antoine that if he should give us one more play of the type of *Lucie Pellegrin*, a certain number of us prefer never again to set foot in his theatre. He knows very well that art has nothing to do with that sort of filth.

Antoine tried to justify himself in a long reply, in which he claimed that he was following his usual custom of opening his doors to young writers. Alexis, he affirmed, was of the Zola school which rightly or wrongly was trying to bring about on the stage the evolution that had been wrought in the novel. If Alexis went astray, that was his own fault. The plays of the Théâtre-Libre were not open to the public. The wives and daughters of guests were not invited. Antoine went on to protest vigorously against the accusation that he was trying to capitalize a scandal. On the contrary, he had risked losing subscribers for the next season by producing *Lucie Pellegrin*. Once more he stoutly resented the charge that the Théâtre-Libre was controlled by the naturalists, and listed the many plays produced there by their opponents. So far as personal support went he assured Sarcey that Mendès had been much more helpful to him than Zola. Although he and his associates might be on the wrong track at times, they were artists and hard workers feeling their way here and there. He reminded Sarcey that he had been among the very first to welcome the dramatic experiment which was the Théâtre-Libre, and that he, Antoine, valued his criticism so highly that he was heartbroken when Sarcey could not praise the efforts of his troupe.

Sarcey published Antoine's reply, which he termed an apology, and assured his readers that the director of the

Théâtre-Libre would never offend them again with a play like *Lucie Pellegrin*. And although Antoine professed to believe in the sincerity of Alexis, he recognized that it would be jeopardizing the future of his theatre to go to such extremes again. Alexis ridiculed Antoine for his letter to Sarcey and accused him of attempting to curry favor with that powerful critic. He referred scathingly to the newly acquired modesty of "Saint" Antoine and made plans to give a public performance of *Lucie Pellegrin* at the Théâtre Dézajet during Antoine's absence in Brussels. Antoine immediately threatened to discharge any member of his company who should appear in a public performance of Alexis's play, and a merry row ensued which was given wide publicity. The upshot was that *Lucie Pellegrin* was not produced publicly, and the enemies of the Théâtre-Libre, who were already beginning to gloat over the disruption of that theatre, were disappointed. Alexis saw the light, withdrew his play from the Dézajet, and remained a loyal supporter of the Théâtre-Libre.

In addition to this unpleasant notoriety, Antoine found himself in debt to the tune of ten thousand francs, a situation which gave the lie to the report that he was enriching himself on scandals. He had decided to move from the Montparnasse theatre in spite of an artistically successful season. It would always be an uphill fight to continue to work in a playhouse so remote from the theatrical centre of Paris. The Menus-Plaisirs on the Boulevard Strasbourg was chosen as the new home of the Théâtre-Libre, and arrangements were made for two monthly performances during the following season, one for representatives of the press, authors, and their friends, another for public subscribers, whose numbers were constantly increasing. The greatest drawback was that scenery had to be furnished at the new theatre; but Antoine saw that his work had begun to arouse discussion on questions of *mise-en-scène*, and, in spite of the additional financial burdens involved, he recognized that the Théâtre-Libre would gain artistically by having its own scenery made for each play. The new theatre had definitely taken its place in the artistic world of Paris. The sculptor Charpentier had executed a medallion of each author who had produced plays at the Théâtre-Libre, and the series, exhibited at the Salon, received a great deal of attention.

There was much discussion during the summer months about the possibility of presenting a dramatization of Flaubert's *Madame Bovary* and Renan's philosophical drama, *L'Abbesse de Jouarre*. Flaubert was so strongly opposed to the presentation of his novel in dramatic form that Antoine dropped the idea. Renan, who had been a little disturbed by the notoriety that the Théâtre-Libre had won, insisted upon an actress of the high calibre of Duse, who had already produced the play in Italy. Antoine, aiming high, went to Sarah Bernhardt, who received the proposal very coldly, and so the project was dropped.

In July, Antoine saw at Brussels some performances of the famous company of the Duke of Meiningen. The quality of the acting of this troupe made a vivid impression on him, and he embodied his ideas in a letter to Sarcey in which he refuted certain statements of Claretie, then director of the Comédie-Française, who also had seen the German company perform. This letter throws so much light upon existing conditions on the French stage, and the ideas expressed in it influenced so much the destinies of the Théâtre-Libre, that I shall quote it almost in full.

I must tell you that I have just come from Brussels where I have spent a fortnight studying that German troupe. You know that I am going to put on *La Patrie en danger* this winter, and in connection with it I had been thinking of trying an interesting experiment with crowds. To go and see the Meininger was then a matter of course. Since I have been going to the theatre I have been annoyed with what we do with our supernumeraries. If I except *La Haine*, and the circus in *Théodora*, I have never seen anything which has given me the sensation of a multitude. Well, I did get that sensation on seeing the Meininger. They showed us things absolutely new and very instructive. Their crowds are not like ours, composed of elements picked haphazard, working-men hired for dress rehearsals, badly clothed, and unaccustomed to wearing strange and uncomfortable costumes, especially when they are exact. Immobility is almost always required of the crowds on our stage, whereas the supernumeraries of the Meininger must act and mime their characters. Don't understand by that that they force the note and that the attention is distracted from the protagonists. No, the tableau is complete, and in whatever direction you may look, you fix your eyes on a detail in the situation or character. At certain moments its power is incomparable.

The troupe of the Meininger contains about seventy actors of both sexes. All those who do not take a part are expected to figure in the play, and every evening too. If there are twenty actors occupied, the fifty others, without a single exception, even in the case of the leading players, appear on the stage in the tableaux, and each leading actor is the chief, the corporal of a group of real supernumeraries, whom he directs and watches as long as the company is under the eye of the public. This obligation is such that the wife of Hans von Bülow, one of the stars of the Meininger, having refused to perform this service, which she considered beneath her talent, was dismissed, although her husband had the title and functions of Kappelmeister to the Duke of Saxony. In this way they obtain ensembles that are extraordinarily true to life. Just try to apply this principle on our stage and demand even of a fifth-rate player that he occupy with his presence the salon of the Princesse de Bouillon! And so we are forced to use worthy people who have no idea of what they are doing on the stage, nor why they are there at all. I know all about it, I used to be a supernumerary at the Comédie-Française with Mévisto. Thus we used to see at close quarters the actors who had roused our enthusiasm when we were in the audience. Well, the Meininger adapt themselves to circumstances. Mlle. Lindner, their star, playing in the *Winter's Tale*, took a silent part in the tableau of the seat of justice, and mimed a woman of the people as conscientiously and as carefully as she interpreted on the following evening the important rôle of Hermione in the same piece. That is the secret of their crowds, which are absolutely superior to ours.

Why should not these new, logical, and not at all costly things eventually replace those insupportable conventions which everybody endures with us without knowing why? The word "mechanical," which M. Claretie has used, does not seem to me very just. Is not everything at the Comédie-Française, where certain works are repeated month after month, arranged mechanically? The mechanics of tableaux are perfected in superior fashion in the crowds of the Meininger, that's the truth. In tableaux, the protagonist who is on the stage can make periods of silence ring true with a gesture, a cry, a movement. And if the crowd listens and looks at the actor instead of looking at the audience, or, as at the Comédie-Française, at the stars, with silent but visible deference, it will be found quite natural that a crowd of two hundred persons should be silent together, listening in rapt attention to a character who interests everybody.

I know nothing about music, but I have been told that in certain operas Wagner divided the choruses into several parts, and that each group of singers personified a distinct element of the crowd, which fused into a perfect ensemble. Why shouldn't we do that on the speaking stage? M. Zola wanted to do it in *Germinal*, but could not because the directors objected on financial grounds. His idea was to have several rehearsals of ensembles led by actors who should take the parts of supernumeraries. You see, that was the procedure of the Meininger. Why shouldn't we try to appropriate for ourselves the best elements of these interesting innovations? I am going to put a little of what I have seen in Brussels into Goncourt's *Patrie en danger* and Hennique's *Mort du duc d'Enghien*.

This letter Sarcey published in the *Temps*. The Théâtre-Libre occupied far more newspaper space than any other theatre in Paris, for two reasons. In the first place, Antoine produced more new plays than any other two theatres, and secondly its plays, when they were not foreign, were either so unconventional or so controversial that they furnished more copy for the critics and "funny colyumists" than all the playhouses of Paris combined. And this was the first season of an amateur company! Antoine had given Paris seventeen new plays, eight long ones and nine short ones — an astonishing total when one considers the infinite care and detail that went into each play, which had only one performance. No matter how successful the play, it had no run, whereas some of the Paris theatres ran one play for a whole season. Hostile critics, who condemned the Théâtre-Libre so roundly, overlooked the fact that, by the law of average, it was impossible to present a masterpiece at each performance. If only one fourth of Antoine's plays were good, he had struck a higher average than that of any other theatre, including those subsidized by the state.

The legitimate theatres not only borrowed Antoine's actors, they retained them, much to his discomfiture. As to his own ability as an actor, the press was unanimous. He had eliminated all the theatricality of the conventional player and inspired in his company the same simplicity and naturalness which characterized his own acting.

What suppleness [writes one critic] he brings into his characters which are so utterly different one from the other! With what surety of composition he succeeds in giving, in the same evening, to most varied rôles, a silhouette so successful that at first one does not recognize him. He never plays Antoine, he always plays his character and, penetrating the soul of his character, he presents him in an unforgettable manner. It is singular, but it seems that there is no stage, and that the raised curtain of the Théâtre-Libre discloses people in their houses going about their affairs unconsciously and without knowing that they are watched.

However much they may have differed in their criticisms of the plays, Lemaître, Faguet, and Sarcey were one in their praise of Antoine's acting, although Sarcey occasionally grumbled because he could not hear him.

Antoine was so bent upon avoiding the mannerisms and poses of the conventional player that he often spoke with his back completely turned to the audience, an unheard-of procedure on the Paris stage of his day. He believed that the play should be performed without thought of an audience, and he exaggerated this tendency to such an extent, even when using a conversational tone, that he could not be heard by his auditors. Thus it was that the nickname "Antoine's Back" became synonymous with Théâtre-Libre. One wag had it that Antoine had a rich uncle who threatened to cut him off from his will if he ever saw him on the stage. "All right," said Antoine, "I 'll go on the stage, but my uncle will never see me." His greatest defect was a weak voice, a defect which he has himself acknowledged and which remains with him even to this day. It is very difficult to hear him in a large hall. This weakness was probably due to the fact that he never received expert training in voice culture. We can, however, overlook this shortcoming when we remember that we have many actors with perfectly trained voices, but only one Antoine.

CHAPTER VI

THE SECOND AND THIRD SEASONS
(1888–1890)

THE season of 1888–1889 was inaugurated by three unconventional one-act plays which gave Antoine an unusual opportunity of showing his audience what he could do with his own stage-settings. The first, *Les Bouchers*, written by a young poet, Fernand Icres, was a combination of realistic plot with romantic verse. It is a bloody tragedy in which two butchers murder each other in a butcher shop, "all for the love of a lady." *Chevalerie rustique*, a French rendering of Verga's *Cavalleria Rusticana*, was interesting mainly because of its picturesque *mise-en-scène*, the real fountain that Antoine introduced, and the ear-biting episode. This play has been temporarily rescued from oblivion by Mascagni's music. Darzens's *Amante du Christ*, a mystery based on the familiar story of Christ and the harlot, stirred up much controversy as to the propriety of introducing the figure of Christ on the stage; but Darzens vowed that he was a good Catholic and had no intention of being irreligious. He handles his situation very delicately and his play contains some beautiful verse. *L'Amante du Christ* was exceedingly well staged and well acted. Darzens started a heated discussion among poets and critics by using the cæsura after the eighth instead of after the sixth syllable in his verse, but disclaimed any originality by pointing out that Richepin, Mendès, Leconte de Lisle, and Coppée had already written verses of that type.

The five acts of Louis de Gramont's *Rolande* filled the entire bill of the November performance, and was one of the most discussed works of the Théâtre-Libre. Gramont was a journalist, poet, and translator of Shakespeare's *Othello*. His *Rolande* was doubtless inspired by the Hulot of Balzac's *Cousine Bette*. Gramont's de Montmorin, outwardly a respectable paterfamilias and member of the Legion of Honor, is so obsessed by the attractions of the fair sex that he stoops to the lowest of crimes. He is finally given a revolver by his daughter, Rolande, with which he puts an end to his life. *Rolande* illustrates the ambition of many playwrights of the latter part of the nineteenth century to dramatize characters of their literary hero, Balzac. The author seems to go out of his way to put crude expressions into the mouths of his characters. He has considerable dramatic power, and had he reduced his play to three acts, he might have succeeded in giving us a powerful tragedy. Lacking the art of elimination, he has left an overstrained and declamatory work. It is an excellent example of the exaggerated tendencies of the so-called naturalist school of drama. Were it not for the Théâtre-Libre, *Rolande* would never have been written.

The next performance brought to the Théâtre-Libre two plays which mark a date in its history, *La Chance de Françoise* (originally entitled *Mariê*) of Porto-Riche, and *La Mort du duc d'Enghien* of Hennique. Porto-Riche's one-act play went from the Théâtre-Libre to the Gymnase and later to the Comédie-Française, where it still remains on the repertory. Marcel Desroches is Porto-

Riche's Don Juan, who appears later in *Le Passé* and *Le Vieil Homme* under different names. In the Théâtre-Libre play it is only Françoise's luck that saves her from her husband's infidelity. Antoine may be called the discoverer and impresario of Porto-Riche,— one of the most distinguished French playwrights, — although *La Chance de Françoise* was not his first play. In *La Chance de Françoise*, there is a little of Marivaux, a little of Musset, with a dash of Becque; but the cruel irony of the latter is tempered with the saving grace of poetry. It is only recently that Porto-Riche, author of *Amoureuse*, one of the masterpieces of modern French playwriting, has won a seat in the Academy, an honor which he owes in no small measure to the pen of his friend and champion, Antoine.

But Porto-Riche's delicate and exquisite study of marital love was momentarily overshadowed by its companion piece, Hennique's *Mort du duc d'Enghien*, which kept the critics busy for several weeks. It is one of the most exaggerated examples in contemporary French drama of a loosely constructed play. It is what the French critic calls a *pièce mal faite*, and it justifies, more than any other play of the Théâtre-Libre, the characterization of free drama. It has nothing whatever in common with the ultra-realist or so-called naturalist drama. It is what we should call an historical pageant, a dramatic form which has not won favor with most French critics. With its beautiful and meticulously exact *mise-en-scène* and costumes, its historical accuracy and its noble appeal, it at first carried the audience off its feet; but when examined minutely in the light of the cold, gray dawn, it showed itself to be merely a spectacle. It belongs, in a way, to the transition between the spoken play and the cinema. It became part of Antoine's travelling repertory and was given a number of public performances. To us, however, its interest is mainly historical. Its author, Hennique, was one of Zola's disciples and one of the warriors of the Théâtre-Libre, and had already produced two of its most successful plays. *La Mort du duc d'Enghien* was a revival of the historical play, without the fustian and bombast of the romantic dramatists. It was, no doubt, influenced by that other pageant, *La Patrie en danger*, of the Goncourts, which was to be produced later in the season by Antoine, and which had been languishing for many years for want of a producer. It is the widest possible swing of the pendulum from the well-made play, the special *bête noire* of Zola and the Goncourts. Hennique calls it a drama in three tableaux. It contains no declamations, no tirades, no attempt to falsify history, but it did not succeed in maintaining itself as drama. In spite of all its excellent points, it is photography and not drama. With the help of André Rivoire of the Chat Noir, the inventor of the famous shadow pictures, Antoine realized certain effects in lighting that had been hitherto unknown in France. In some of the scenes the footlights were extinguished and all the light came from candles and lanterns used on the stage. This was an innovation that excited no end of discussion in Paris dramatic circles.

The influence of the Théâtre-Libre was beginning to make itself felt in many of the theatres of Paris. We have seen how several of its plays found their way to the public playhouses. Porel had been watching closely the work of the Théâtre-Libre, and not wishing to be left behind by the new movement, produced at the Odéon about this time a dramatization of Goncourt's *Germinie Lacerteux*.

"Antoine has moved to the Odéon," exclaimed the
critics. Here was a public performance of a play of the
ultra-realist type given at a national theatre. Not even
the superb acting of Réjane, however, could save *Germinie
Lacerteux* from being howled down by the audience. The
press was almost unanimously hostile.

This was the kind of thing that was dear to Antoine's
heart. The smoke of dramatic battles was meat and
drink to him. He impetuously dashed off a note to Bauer,
one of the champions of the Théâtre-Libre and one of the
few defenders of Goncourt's dramatized novels, saying
that the reception accorded to *Germinie Lacerteux* had
impelled him to advance the date of the performance of
La Patrie en danger. He would like to see whether those
"damned idiots" would try any of their "rough stuff"
on him.

An indiscreet secretary published this note, which was
pounced upon by the critics, who threatened to make
Antoine eat his words. They were so incensed at the
epithet *gueux d'imbéciles*, which became a *mot* in Paris,
that Antoine judged it prudent to explain that he was
not referring to the critics but to the rowdy element in
the audience. It was a very lame excuse, and Antoine,
much worried by the tempest he had created, went to
consult the editor of the *Figaro*, who ridiculed him for his
fears. "What! you are hauled over the coals three times
on the front page of the *Figaro* and yet you complain?"
All this hubbub of course linked Antoine more and more
closely with Zola's group, and once embarked on a campaign of championing plays like *Germinie Lacerteux*,
which had not even been played at his theatre, he found
it increasingly difficult to get support from the enemies
of the naturalists.

The New Year was ushered in, however, with a poetic drama of Mendès which offered a sort of antidote to the *Germinie Lacerteux* episode, and the threat of a public apology, which it had been intimated would be exacted of Antoine, was forgotten. *La Reine Fiammette*, in six acts, originally written for Bernhardt, was the last-born child of the romantic school. Done in the spirit of the elder Dumas and Victor Hugo, it contains many beautiful verses. It has found its true place in operatic form, where the music of Xavier Leroux has toned down its lasciviousness. Antoine had serious doubts with regard to *La Reine Fiammette*, but he produced it for two reasons. First, Mendès, who had been an ardent supporter of the Théâtre-Libre since its inception, had repeatedly urged him to do so; and, secondly, he was glad of another opportunity to prove that he was not bound by theories and schools. It was a difficult undertaking for him financially, as the settings and costumes were very costly. Coming right on the heels of another expensive play, *La Mort du duc d'Enghien*, it put him considerably in debt. Antoine himself was very roughly handled by the critics, who were still smarting from his lashing, and they pummelled him unmercifully for attempting to play the rôle of a Renaissance king. And they were justified. Antoine was not felicitous in parts requiring distinguished and noble bearing. He excelled in what we popularly call character parts, especially middle-aged and old men. He was not cut out by nature to play the part of the dashing and elegant *jeune premier*.

With the next play, we go back once more to the realists. Céard, the author of *Les Résignés*, was, like Hennique and Alexis, one of the Médan five. *Les Résignés* is one of

the most literary plays in the history of the Théâtre-
Libre, and shows strongly the influence of Dumas fils and
Becque. It has the chiselled phraseology of Dumas and the
cruel cynicism of Becque. The characters are not living
people, they lack frankness and naturalness. They have
the air of professional psychologists analyzing one another. Henriette and Bernard are in love with each other
but cannot marry because of his meagre salary. Bernard
would have Henriette marry a literary friend, but her
aunt offers her a prosperous bookseller. In the end she
marries neither, and has to be resigned to Bernard, now
not only poor but also wrecked in health after a long ill-
ness. The plot is unimportant; it serves merely as a peg
on which to hang brilliant repartee and cruel reciprocal
probings. *Les Résignés* is a play in which each character
lays the other on Zola's dissecting table and uses the
literary scalpel with a vengeance. Its companion piece,
Jullien's second play, *L'Echéance*, is a monologue in one
act, in which a banker on the verge of bankruptcy winks
at his wife's relations with a rich admirer who furnishes
the funds that are needed to save her husband from disaster.

La Patrie en danger of the Goncourts, for which *La
Mort du duc d'Enghien* was only a trial balloon, was not
so well received as Antoine had anticipated. It has an
interesting history. Written by the brothers Goncourt in
1868, it had been refused at the Comédie-Française for
political reasons. The officials of Napoleon III could
hardly be expected to sanction a play which glorified
revolution. Published in 1873, it had to wait until 1889
for its first presentation on the boards. It was looked
upon by the authors, specialists in eighteenth-century

civilization, as an experiment in historical drama. Long before Zola, the Goncourts had been up in arms against the popular historical play. *La Patrie en danger* is, like *La Mort du duc d'Enghien*, a pageant in five tableaux. The French who have given us the word pageant, have no word themselves which describes this dramatic genre. Edmond de Goncourt was intensely disliked by the critics and they tore his play to pieces.

With its vivid pictures of crowds, its pictorial beauty, *La Patrie en danger* is an excellent pageant, but a pageant that is spoiled by a meticulous literary flavor. Filled with interminable and pedantic dialogues, exact in every detail, reproducing minutely language and historical event, it smacks too much of the study. In spite of its beautiful and poetic style, it is wearisome. Both Lemaître and Faguet, who on many an occasion championed the plays of the Théâtre-Libre in the face of almost unanimous opposition, found *La Patrie en danger* impossible as drama. Sarcey said that he was severer with the Goncourts than with others because they claimed to have founded a new school of drama, and had led astray many a young dramatist. As to the introduction of the five hundred moving, shouting supernumeraries, so dear to Antoine's heart, the critics insisted that five or six would have sufficed, inasmuch as the crowd had to be silent during the long dialogue of the principals. As was the case with *La Mort du duc d'Enghien*, Antoine suppressed the footlights and brought his light from above, a most heretical innovation in France then, but one which has been gradually adopted in all the theatres of the advance guard in Paris to-day. In general, the Goncourts showed themselves to be, as always, excellent stylists, accurate historians, but inferior playwrights; *La Patrie en danger* is dramatic caviar. Much against his will, Antoine was persuaded by Derembourg of the Menus-Plaisirs to give a series of public performances of *La Patrie en danger*, but it never attained the popularity of *La Mort du duc d'Enghien*.

All the glory of the performance was due to Antoine. As Bauer said,

In spite of jealousies, polemics, grudges, and insults, Antoine pursues his task indefatigably. Although he may have moments of awkwardness, he knows long hours of patient study and intelligent work. Whatever may be said to the contrary, this improvised director has given us new and interesting plays. This time again, he has the honor of having had the happy audacity to assume, with his modest resources and humble means, an enterprise before which all directors have recoiled for twenty years, namely the *mise-en-scène* of *La Patrie en danger*.

After the Goncourts came Zola, with a long-forgotten play, *Madeleine*, which dated back to 1865. Contrary to the usual procedure, Zola had written the play long before the novel *Madeleine Férat*, which had been based upon it. He purposely did not retouch it, and gave it to Antoine because the latter had repeatedly asked him for a play of his own. Like all of Zola's dramatic work, it has nothing in common with his dramatic theories. It is full of outworn *clichés* and does credit to the author only in the characterization of Madeleine Férat, who, like Thérèse Raquin, is made to suffer the tortures of remorse. Contrary to expectation, the critics took Zola at his word, namely, that he had presented *Madeleine* merely as an historical specimen, and so they dealt very gently with him. Sarcey ventured to suggest, and very patly, that had Zola persisted in writing plays and in studying the art of the drama at a time when he had no theories and prejudices, he might have become a great play-wright. It is curious that Zola should have permitted the presentation of a play so diametrically opposed to all the theories which he had been so vigorously promulgating. But he seems to have had an obsession for seeing crea-tures of his fancy upon the stage, and was willing to in-dulge in that vanity at a time when he felt that his literary reputation could not be injured by an amateurish work of his youth. It is significant that *Madeleine*, the play, does not figure among Zola's published works.

The Théâtre-Libre was fast becoming a museum of *pièces inédites*. After Zola and the Goncourts, came Léon Cladel with his one-act tragedy in verse, *L'Ancien*, venerable in years, but utterly lacking in interest. It was Ancey's second play, *Les Inséparables*, the companion piece to *L'Ancien*, which engaged the attention of the audience. Witty, spontaneous, and cynical, it seemed, like *M. Lamblin*, to herald greater things from the young playwright. The inseparables are Gaston and Paul, the lamb and the wolf. Cécile first accepts the lamb, but is immediately seized by the wolf, who hands her back to the lamb when he finds that she is not so rich as she had been rated. But the lamb is not to have full pos-session of Cécile. The wolf does not completely relin-quish his prey. We are led to infer that the lady is destined to become his mistress. Why was it that the brilliant, scintillating Ancey never reached the front rank of playwrights? Was it that he became imprisoned by the formulas of the "naturalists" and gradually exaggerated his rather ferocious humor and cold-blooded cynicism until it, in turn, became as much of a convention as the conventional type of play which he was combating? The

Théâtre-Libre, in allowing Ancey to give full rein to his
cynical bent, injured rather than helped him. The conventional theatre might have filed Ancey's over-sharp-
ened claws.

The last programme of the season 1888–1889 is interesting to us Americans because it contained an adaptation of Baudelaire's translation of one of Poe's stories,
Tell-Tale Heart, a gruesome, hair-raising confession of
murder in the form of a dramatic monologue. Méténier's
Casserole is another of those sensational one-act *tranches
de vie* popularly regarded as belonging exclusively to the
Théâtre-Libre movement. *La Casserole* — Apache slang
for police denunciator — is like Méténier's *En Famille*,
a picture of the Paris underworld. Stage realism reached
its height in the appearance of a real juggler and heavy-
weight artist among the cast. Antoine himself admitted
that this sort of dramatized police record was getting to
be tiresome.

The second season ended with a "dud," but it had
firmly established the Théâtre-Libre as the leading playhouse of the advance guard in Paris, just as the Comédie-
Française was the leading theatre of the conventional
play. It had become the battleground for new types of
plays, new ideas in stage-setting, and new ideas in lighting. Critics like Lemaître, Faguet, and Sarcey defended
Antoine against the fierce onslaughts of Hector Plessard,
who, in the preface of *Annales du théâtre et de la musique*
for the current year, made ridiculous accusations against
Antoine and the Théâtre-Libre. Antoine had certainly
given the lie to the charge that the Théâtre-Libre was the
dramatic nursery of the "naturalist" movement, by presenting such plays as *L'Amante du Christ, La Chance de*

Françoise, Le Cor fleuri, La Reine Fiammette, and *La Mort du duc d'Enghien.* He admitted that *La Patrie en danger, Madeleine,* and *L'Ancien* were mere literary curiosities. But to the warm defence of the Théâtre-Libre by Bauer, who, paraphrasing Zola, said that the "Théâtre-Libre will be naturalist or it will not be," the young director replied:

I am not entirely of that opinion. I think that too narrow a formula would mean death, and that, on the contrary, we must be ready to receive everybody broadly. I feel very strongly that already at the Rue Blanche we are getting to be a little chapel; the old guard of the Théâtre-Libre is becoming disturbed by my eclecticism. This is a critical turning point in the road for me; I must manœuvre between Bauer, who is always ready to show his ill humor when he isn't listened to enough, and Mendès, whose hold is more clever and more insinuating but none the less dangerous.

The third season, of 1889–1890, opened with a play in verse by Jean Aicard, *Le Père Lebonnard.* It had been accepted by the Comédie-Française, but the author had been so harassed by the criticisms on the part of the administration and actors that he had withdrawn it. Antoine, scenting an opportunity to present a disputed play which was conspicuously not of the "naturalist" school, offered his theatre to Aicard. *Le Père Lebonnard* was preceded at the Théâtre-Libre by a prologue, *Dans le Guignol,* in which Aicard rather ineffectually satirized the director and actors of the Comédie-Française. Although the announcement of this prologue created a mighty stir in the dramatic world of Paris, it fell flat. Aicard was a romantic poet, not a satirist, and to-day *Dans le Guignol* is regarded as a tame skirmish in the battle between the leading conventional and unconventional theatres of Paris. As for *Le Père Lebonnard* itself, it is a sentimental bit of bourgeois romantic philosophy tinged with socialism. Sylvain, a venerable *sociétaire* of the Comédie-Française, resurrected it some years later, and it now forms part of the repertory of that theatre. The whole affair was but an adventure in the history of the Théâtre-Libre, and had no influence in its development.

With the performance of Ancey's *École des veufs*, the Théâtre-Libre found itself once more in the thick of the combat. *L'École des veufs* is one of the most pronounced specimens of dramatic *rosserie* produced at the Théâtre-Libre. It is a scabrous, witty portrait of a senile father who takes a young mistress into his house very soon after the death of his wife. He is so infatuated with this pretty adventuress that he is willing to share her with a rival, his own son. Once more Ancey shows the influence of Becque, a ribald Becque. The dialogue, though lively and comic, is too indecent to win success on the public stage. Ancey is at his best in ironical passages like the following, which might be considered the immoral moral of the play. "When men have not with them a woman of tact and modesty who watches over them in their lives, the family is but a body without a head, a ship without a compass."

The first act, really a prologue, is a parody of a funeral, showing all the hypocrisies attached to it. The last four acts, like Becque's *Parisienne*, have but three characters, the father, the son, and the prostitute. The struggle for the possession of the woman results in a draw. It is a *rosse* burlesque of the *ménage à trois* in the spirit of Becque's *Parisienne* and Brieux's *Hannetons*. Antoine said of *L'École des veufs:*

This is certainly, since Becque, the freshest, the most audacious, and at the same time the most classic of plays. . . . It is the first time perhaps that I have realized the power of the unconsciously comic. This or that word might be revolting if it were uttered by the actor as if he actually realized the enormities that he is saying; it becomes a prodigious bit of drollery when it comes spontaneously from the character. I am discovering that the Théâtre-Libre, without premeditation on the part of any of us, by mere devotion to the sense and spirit of its plays, is in process of creating something new in the acting of the comedian.

L'École des veufs is a brilliant example of the modern *esprit gaulois* and follows the tradition of the mediæval *fabliau* and the Molièresque farce.

Turgenev's *Pain d'autrui* was the weakest of the foreign plays produced at the Théâtre-Libre. The author was never successful as a dramatist and his play had been a failure in Russia. Antoine's acting of the parasite Vasili was the redeeming feature of the performance. Porto-Riche's one-act play in verse, *L'Infidèle*, was to have been performed at the same time, but was withdrawn by the author because of Coquelin's refusal to take the principal part. *Les Frères Zemganno* of the Goncourts, dramatized by Alexis and Méténier, was, like *Sœur Philomène* of the same authors, merely a series of tableaux taken from the novel.

Brieux's début at the Théâtre-Libre was his *Ménages d'artistes*, a clumsy melodrama in which the author already showed his tendency to try to better social conditions. It was completely overshadowed by Jean Jullien's *Maître*, the last play of this writer produced at the Théâtre-Libre. It shows very patently Jullien's efforts to tone down his language and situations. The first tableau of this "étude de paysans," as the author calls it, would make an excellent one-act play; the last two tab-

leaux are weak. They are full of the old stage tricks and
fail to present a carefully worked-out study of the
peasants. *Le Maître* was performed later on the legitimate stage, but never imposed itself. Jullien, who had
been one of a half-dozen first-class playwrights of the
ultra-realistic school, had come to the parting of the
ways. During the later years of the Théâtre-Libre he
never missed an occasion to criticize Antoine most
harshly, and although his own *Sérénade* was one of the
most extreme plays of this theatre, he constantly accused
the Théâtre-Libre of being conventionally indecent.

One of the most popular successes of the Théâtre-
Libre was *La Tante Léontine* of Boniface and Bodin.
Antoine considered it one of the most daring pieces he
had yet produced, and explained its popularity on the
ground that its realistic elements were so skilfully disguised with farce that they passed unnoticed. *La Tante
Léontine* is a wealthy retired prostitute who wishes to
dower her impoverished niece in return for the cloak of
respectability which her brother's respectable family will
give her. Although its general theme is daring enough, it
has a certain reticence of language which won praise for
it even from the most puritanical critics. In point of construction it was so conventional that it found great favor
in the eyes of Sarcey, who offered to help the authors
find a place for it on the commercial stage.

About this time, April, 1890, Antoine felt that at last
the influence of the Théâtre-Libre was percolating
through to the other theatres of Paris. Alexis and Méténier with *Monsieur Betsy*, Ancey with his *Grand'Mère*,
and Hennique with his *Amour* found themselves accepted
by the Variétés and the Odéon. Porel had not only taken

Jacques Damour from the Théâtre-Libre, but had produced *Amour* and *Grand'Mère* as well as the much-discussed *Germinie Lacerteux*, and he was in each case
severely handled by the conservative critics. They had
begun to set up danger signals and had warned the public
that the influence of the Théâtre-Libre was contaminat-
ing French drama. Antoine read these warnings with
great glee.

> I have the impression [he says] that the horizon is beginning to be
> transformed, but at the Rue Blanche we are very sanguine when we
> imagine that the doors have been forced. At each success that is
> somewhat spectacular, they seem to stand ajar, but at the slightest
> faltering, we are escorted out. That situation will last, I feel it more
> than anyone else, years and years. For the moment everything smiles
> about us, the year seems to be ending in a burst of glory.

He warned his young enthusiasts nevertheless not to be
too hopeful for immediate victory, and he quoted one
critic who said: "It may be true that the Théâtre-Libre
hasn't given us good plays, but it makes us consider bad
most of the plays produced elsewhere."

After Tolstoy, Ibsen. *Ghosts*, with the *Power of Darkness*, *Les Corbeaux*, Strindberg's *Miss Julia*, and their
prototype, Zola's *Thérèse Raquin*, formed the bible of the
ultra-realist playwrights of Europe. Ibsen's play had been
censored in Germany and in England, and was the opening shot fired in the dramatic battles of the Freie Bühne
in Berlin and the Independent Theatre in London, both
offshoots of the Théâtre-Libre. Antoine had been thinking
about *Ghosts* since August, 1888, when he mentioned it
in his letter to Sarcey as forming part of the repertory of
of the Duke of Meiningen's company. In January, 1890,
Zola called Antoine's attention to an article on *Ghosts*,
which had made a rumpus in Germany, and urged An-

toine to play it. Antoine was naturally anxious not to fall
behind the German and English free theatres, but post-
poned its production because he was not satisfied with
a French translation which had been made from a German version of the original. Most of his little inner circle
opposed its presentation. Mendès found it "impossible";
Céard considered that it was "totally incomprehensible to
our Latin brains," and advised prefacing it with a prologue; Ancey pronounced it "magnificent," but suggested cuts. Finally, Darzens got some expert help and
prepared an entirely new translation of the Norwegian
original, which was submitted to Ibsen himself. All of
which shows the painstaking care and love for dramatic
detail which reigned at the Rue Blanche as well as the
openmindedness and dramatic *flair* of the leader there.

But in spite of all this precaution, the critics, for the
most part, found *Ghosts* vague, dull, and prolix. Antoine,
who had played Oswald, was on the contrary thrilled
by the part. Shortly after the performance, he wrote:

> I experienced a sensation hitherto unknown to me, the almost
> complete loss of my own personality. From the beginning of the sec-
> ond act, I remembered nothing, neither the public, nor the effect of
> the performance, and when the curtain fell, I found myself shudder-
> ing, enervated, incapable of pulling myself together for some mo-
> ments.

Needless to say that, unlike the English and German
critics, the French did not prate about the immorality
of *Ghosts:* they found it foggy. Is it a pose on the part of
the French to consider everything that comes from
northern Europe lacking in clarity? "A Zola with a
wooden leg," was one critic's characterization of Ibsen.
Perhaps French audiences cannot understand the coldness and aloofness of Ibsen. His lack of passion and em-

phasis, his unwillingness to make telling points in his dialogue, were so foreign to their nature that they found him enigmatic. Another reason perhaps for the inability of the French to comprehend Ibsen is his deadly seriousness. French writers often go out of their way to explain to English-speaking peoples and Germans that they are essentially moralists, but that it is not necessary to be gloomy to be a moralist. There were, happily, exceptions to the chorus of disapproval. Faguet felt that *Ghosts* was clumsily constructed but was "one of the half dozen greatest dramas of the century." Paul Desjardins hailed Ibsen "the greatest living dramatist." And Lemaître, the least chauvinist of French critics, who had been one of the very first to write about Ibsen in France, although pronouncing *Ghosts* a "beautiful and strong tragedy which shakes our soul," yet found it "strange to our clear heads. . . . *Ghosts* needs explanation. It must be studied."

One would think that, with his stark realism, his simplicity of construction, his utter scorn for dramatic theories, Ibsen would have pleased the iconoclastic audience of the Théâtre-Libre. On the contrary, it found him boresome. And despite all that Antoine has done for Ibsen in France, despite the later efforts of Lugné-Poe, the Norwegian dramatist who, after Zola, has been the most potent influence in contemporary drama, has made little or no impression on the French. Yet in the teeth of almost unanimous opposition, Antoine, who in *Ghosts* had given France its first performance of Ibsen, began to lay plans for the presentation of the *Wild Duck*.

It was unfortunate that Antoine could not have closed his season with the brilliant failure of *Ghosts*. Bergerat's

Myrane was just such a play as one might have seen at any boulevard theatre, but *Les Chapons* of Descaves and Darien created a tremendous hubbub which did not help the Théâtre-Libre. It no longer needed the kind of notoriety furnished by this play. The last performance of the preceding year had shocked Paris because of its immorality, *Les Chapons* was condemned because of its unpatriotic note. Descaves had been severely censured for his *Sous-Offs*, a satire on army life, and had narrowly escaped imprisonment. In *Les Chapons*, the scene is laid at Versailles during the German occupation. The Barbiers have three Prussians quartered with them. Egged on by a friend, and fearing an indiscretion on the part of an old servant, they dismiss her, scantily clothed, in a pouring rain. As she goes, husband and wife engage in the following dialogue:

> "Just look. Is it possible?"
> "What?"
> "Are they [the Prussians] going to drill in weather like this?"
> "Certainly."
> "The poor fellows."

Patriotic feelings apart, this brutal touch is inartistic and puerile. Two French people might possibly say such things to each other in the presence of a German officer, in order to curry favor, but they would never do so in private. This "naturalism" is too unnatural. Coming so soon after the Franco-Prussian War, *Les Chapons* acted like salt on an unhealed wound and goaded the audience into an uproar which lasted nearly half an hour. Antoine was hissed and howled down as he tried to name the authors of the play in accordance with the usual custom. Torrents of ink flowed in condemnation of *Les Chapons*, and the real merits of Antoine's achievements during the dramatic season which had just ended were lost sight of.

Besides the heated arguments over *Les Chapons* and *Le Père Lebonnard*, Antoine became entangled in two controversies of a more personal nature, one with the veteran critic of the *Figaro*, Albert Wolff, who had long been hostile to the Théâtre-Libre, and the other with Bauer of the *Echo de Paris*, who had befriended Antoine from the very start. The second quarrel was more serious than the first, and involved Antoine in a lawsuit, in which he sued his former friend for defamation of character. It all arose from the fact that Antoine refused to produce a play by a friend of Bauer. Antoine finally lost his case, but consoled himself with the statement that the "Théâtre-Libre is a battle, and a house like this cannot live except in a passionate atmosphere." The atmosphere of the season which had just closed was as passionate as the most impassioned fighter could have wished. In fact, it could have well been more artistic and less passionate. In general, the year was far less brilliant than the one which had preceded it.

Towards the close of the theatrical season there appeared in the *Revue des Deux Mondes* an article by Brunetière on the contemporary drama of France, which was not so hostile to the Théâtre-Libre as one might expect from that most dogmatic of critics. Brunetière explains to his readers that for the nth time the question of reform of the drama is on the carpet. Young dramatists once more accuse critics and directors of injustice to them. As for the directors, they must look upon the drama from a financial point of view, and even the Comédie-Française and the Odéon cannot run the risk of financial fail-

ure. As to the critics, whose duty it is to light the way
and prepare the tastes of the public in advance, they have
been slow and lazy and rebellious. The young critics who
maintain that there is only one actor in Paris, Antoine,
and only three authors, Hennique, Ancey, and Jullien,
betray strange confidence in themselves. They think it is
cowardly to make concessions to the elementary laws of
drama, and hurt their case by going to extremes, although much of their criticism against the conventional
play of to-day is just. Young dramatists have gone out
of their way in search of abnormal types. Now the abnormal may succeed in the novel, but we cannot have exceptional characters in the play; they must be general,
and understood by the crowds. Ancey, Hennique, and
Jullien have not made clear their motives. Do they want
the audience to laugh, weep, or to think? Brunetière, like
Sarcey, was much mystified by our young extremists, who
were standing on their heads trying to be unconventional.
The two critics were always afraid that the whole thing
might prove to be a mere hoax. These fears were not so
groundless as they may seem. Parisians are extremely
fond of this form of literary *blague*, and Jean Cocteau and
his band of *dadaïstes* came very near getting away with
a clever hoax on the Paris critics only a few years ago.

Brunetière's greatest quarrel with most of the Théâtre-
Libre writers was that, according to him, they had not
mastered their art. The superstition against the well-
made play and their horror for everything Scribian
worked against them. Their creations are studies,
sketches, but not plays. A play must have action and
plot, otherwise it will be absorbed by the novel. Dramatic
action is what the public wants at the theatre. It can find

character drawing in the works of moralists and essayists, and descriptions, manners, and passions in the novel. All these things may enter into the play, but when the axiomatic law of the struggle is violated, then you have no play. Without this law you cannot interest your general public. When compared with the bitter and violent things that Brunetière found to say against Zola and the Goncourts, this attitude toward the young dramatists was almost praise. Indeed, Antoine so construed it and regarded it as an extremely important indication of the way the tide was turning.

CHAPTER VII

ANTOINE'S DREAM

A T THE close of the season of 1889–1890 there was a deficit of some 12,000 francs; but deficits had a way of rolling off Antoine's back like water off the proverbial duck, and there appeared in May a brochure of about 200 pages in which Antoine sums up the work of the Théâtre-Libre and dreams a dream for the future. This rare brochure is one of the most important documents in the history of the Théâtre-Libre and answers three questions. Why was the Théâtre-Libre needed? What had it done during the three years of its existence? Why must it have a new playhouse? The second question has already been answered in the preceding chapters. The answer to the first presents a most searching criticism of the French stage of the eighteen-eighties and nineties, and the answer to the third gives a detailed and elaborate plan for a model theatre.

This is the burden of Antoine's song: dramatic production in Paris has been in the control of some fifteen playwrights, who monopolize the stage, and who keep writing plays made up of the same ingredients, but with different titles, which pass from one theatre to another. Each author has his own peculiar brand of play, which gradually loses in force as the hand of the author gets heavy with age. But the public is getting weary of this sort of thing and wants something new. This something new we have tried to give in the plays performed during the past three years. But to continue our work we must have a playhouse of our own. Our theatres are uncomfortable and unsafe, witness the terrible fire at the Opéra-Comique, in which so many people lost their lives because of the faulty construction of the building. Such things as newspapers, cheap transportation, and manufactured articles have come within the reach of people of modest means, but the theatres are still a luxury. Then again the system of stars has wrought havoc with our acting. A few good actors surrounded by incompetents is the rule in most of our theatres, and the work of our playwrights is completely deformed by such acting. The new Théâtre-Libre will try to give plays with new ideas, performed by a well-balanced company of actors, in a comfortable playhouse, at reasonable prices.

In spite of violent opposition, the Théâtre-Libre has in three years taken in 120,000 francs and inspired more than 12,000 articles in newspapers and magazines and has been the model for similar organizations in Germany and in England. Fifty-one authors, forty-two of them under forty, have found hospitality at the Théâtre-Libre, and it has had the honor of giving to the Comédie-Française, the Odéon, and the Gymnase several plays from its repertory. After considerable wandering, it now finds the Menus-Plaisirs too small and insufficient for the demands made upon it. It has been compelled to refuse over two hundred subscribers each year during the past two seasons.

The Théâtre-Libre was founded by young men for young men. It is a place where they have been able to give free rein to all sorts of paradoxical effervescences with the uncompromising stubbornness of youth. It has been a hard struggle to fight against commercialism and to maintain the Théâtre-Libre as a literary playhouse open to artists and men of letters. The organizer and director (Antoine always uses the third person) has sought no personal gain in his labors, but finds that the Théâtre-Libre is no longer in an experimental stage and must enlarge its scope. It has won for itself a place in the artistic life of Paris, yet young dramatists have the right to expect to receive financial remuneration for their plays in addition to moral recompense. For a long time Antoine thought that his work was destined to retain its present form — a simple laboratory where young authors, after perfecting their art and enlarging their conceptions, would be received at the regular theatres and thus replace their elders. Antoine asked only to fulfill that modest part, considering himself satisfied with putting young playwrights on their way. But it has been found necessary to give up that Utopian scheme because, from the very first success of the Théâtre-Libre, a coalition has been formed against the new venture. The directors of theatres where works of literary merit are produced, and for which the Théâtre-Libre ought to be a sort of nursery and practical conservatory, have either openly or secretly declared themselves hostile to the new-comers who have wanted to go to them, and have shut their doors in their faces. The rare instances where these authors have been admitted have been due to the insistence of the press or to the unquestioned superiority of the young writers to the men of the old school. And so the merry circus goes on; mediocre playwrights get a hearing because they pay for the honor, and new-comers are forced to produce their plays without royalties.

Now the Théâtre-Libre must continue to fight its battle, so that this present generation of playwrights may not be forced to abandon the struggle and turn to newspaper or book as a means of earning their livelihood. It is absolutely essential that, when they write a good play, it shall be received and played in a house where they will be neither robbed nor strangled. The hostility toward the Théâtre-Libre has grown in proportion to its success. As the sympathy of the press and of men of letters has increased, all the theatrical world that lives at the expense of authors, actors, and public, has fought a relentless war against it. A single exception must be made in the case of the Vaudeville, whose directors have not only loaned actors to the Théâtre-Libre, but have even helped it with subscriptions. The Théâtre-Libre would have succumbed long ago had it not been for the powerful support of the press and its honorary members. Through all the literary polemics (and Antoine is not exaggerating when he speaks of 12,000 articles) the Parisian press has never abandoned the little house which it brought into being. Never have the honorary members of the Théâtre-Libre wavered in their solicitude for the enterprise, which they consider theirs, since for three years they have made it possible.

Theatres are plentiful in Paris, one might even say too plentiful, as they are only half filled each night in spite of changes of bill. A new one would then be superfluous, unless it could be a model house in which the spectator might find comfort and security from danger. The circular form of the Paris theatre condemns two thirds of the spectators in the balconies to be placed, literally and without any exaggeration, opposite each

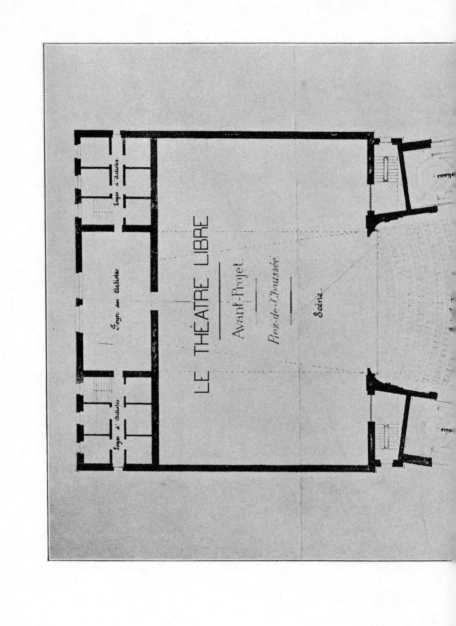

LE THÉATRE LIBRE

Avant-Projet.

Rez-de-Chaussée.

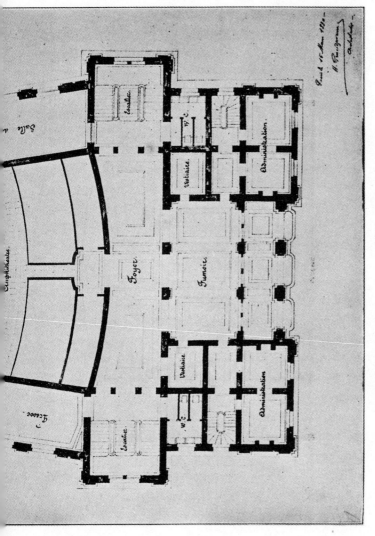

SECOND FLOOR PLAN FOR THE DREAM THEATRE

other. The dramatic action is followed only by a painful turn of the neck. If the people in the first row can see by torturing themselves, those of the back rows are obliged to stand up and project themselves into space in order to see a small part of the stage. It is also true that in the two upper balconies there are whole series of seats from which absolutely nothing can be seen. (One might add parenthetically that the same conditions still persist in most of the Parisian theatres to-day.) It is safe to say then that out of 1200 spectators only 600 can see the play in its entirety, and 400 cannot hear what is said. The Comédie-Française, one of the best equipped of our theatres, is a striking example of the foregoing defects. The circular form of theatre is illogical and contrary to reason.

The spectator, badly placed, is still more badly installed in narrow, hot, dusty, and uncomfortable seats, which are hard to reach. The corridors are poorly ventilated, insufficient, and encumbered with cloak-rooms served by a tyrannical and disagreeable personnel. And for these discomforts one pays dearly. People of modest means must stand in line for hours and get the left-over seats, and are at the mercy of the clerks who dispense them. It is without doubt that because of these purely material considerations, the theatrical business is passing through a crisis.

An attempt to remedy existing conditions will not be successful unless a house is built which will benefit the poorly placed spectator. We must concern ourselves with the thousandth auditor. We must not only give him a place where he can sit without breaking his kneecaps — we must put the spectacle that he has come to see in front of him, and not to his right or to his left. If we keep the balconies in their present form, that is to say, if we place the auditor above the picture, even if he is facing it, he can see only the floor of the stage, and in some cases only the top of the head and a foreshortened figure of the actor. We are inclined then to suppress balconies, all side seats, boxes, and *baignoires*. This is the principle of the theatre of Bayreuth of which the ground plan is given herewith — a single inclined plane with boxes in the rear. This ampitheatre is to seat 800 to 1000 people.

There must be foyers on each side of the auditorium, with wide entrances to them. Upstairs there will be well-ventilated smoking-rooms, reading-rooms, and a café, where one can read, smoke, telegraph, or telephone. A separate room will be maintained for the press from which the critic may telephone his "story." The present cloak-room system must be abolished. Each seat will be provided with a contrivance for wraps. The spectator will be given a numbered ticket at the time of purchase. (A simple scheme, certainly, but one which does not yet prevail in many of the theatres of Paris.) An automatic device will close all the doors of the auditorium as soon as the curtain goes up, so that the spectators and actors will not be disturbed by late-comers.

The execution of this plan will be put in the hands of a young architect, M. Henri Grandpierre, who, with the assistance of Alexandre Charpentier, the sculptor, and M. Albert Vaillant for the mechanical effects, will realize the ambition of Antoine. The building will be fireproof, and the plans have received the approval of M. Eiffel, the well-known engineer and constructor of the Eiffel Tower. The model theatre will be well ventilated and will permit the actors to rehearse in the sunshine and fresh air and not in the vitiated, dark atmosphere of the normal theatre.

So much for the practical side. What about the plays and players? The Comédie-Française and the Odéon received about one million francs in subsidies during the years 1887–1890, and produced only twenty-five and sixty-seven new acts respectively, whereas the Théâtre-Libre produced one hundred and twenty-five during the same period. (It must be kept in mind, however, that the Théâtre-Libre performed new plays exclusively.) As for actors, those of the Théâtre-Libre have been, with a few exceptions, amateurs. In *The Power of Darkness*, for instance, in which the quality of the acting was unanimously praised by the critics, there were two clerks, an architect, a chemist, a travelling salesman, a wine-merchant, a manufacturer, a dressmaker, a bookbinder, and a post-office employee. All rehearsals were held at night. These amateur actors had also faced foreign audiences in London and Brussels, and had been treated as professionals. Some ten have passed on to the professional stage, five of them having been taken by the Odéon. All this leads one to believe that it would be possible to build up a first-class troupe of professional actors without any difficulty whatsoever. If, then, a group of disinterested individuals, by means of their good-will and intelligence, have been able in three years to interpret such widely different characters as those of *Le Baiser*, *L'École des veufs*, and *The Power of Darkness*, is it not just to state that the present official instruction, especially at the *Conservatoire*, is useless and badly conducted?

Antoine then makes a very searching criticism of the *Conservatoire*, a school of drama and music maintained

by the state, where admission was gained by examination
and competition. It will be remembered that he himself
had been refused admission. As for the teachers, continues Antoine, they could not be improved. Got, De-
launay, Maubant, and Worms were the best masters
available in France, but each student received only about
ten hours of personal attention a year from these ex-
perts. Then again the teaching is limited to a small number of scenes from classic plays and rôles are assigned
indifferently to all temperaments. It is possible for a
student to work on a single part for three years, and on
the strength of that, win the *grand prix*, and be elected
to the troupe of the Comédie-Française. Students are not
admitted on the basis of their merits but through influence. It is impossible for the most gifted young man to
enter the *Conservatoire* unless he has backing of some kind.
There are at present ten *premier prix* who are out of a
job and who would not be taken at any theatre in Paris.
One of the teachers at the *Conservatoire* recognizes the
value of the Théâtre-Libre as a school of acting, and
sends students to it because he believes that the only
real test of acting is to face the public. In view of the
hoped-for generation of new playwrights, there will be
needed a new generation of actors. For plays full of observation of life, keen and quick-witted persons will be necessary. A drama that is not based on half a dozen conventional types will need more subtle and intelligent players.
Leading men will, for instance, cease to be all of one
piece, and must become in turn, good, bad, foolish, witty,
elegant, commonplace, strong, weak, brave, and cowardly. The art of acting, will not rest, as at present, on
physical qualities and on natural gifts, but on truth, ob-

servation, and direct study of nature. Just as in painting, the landscape artist no longer works in his studio but in the open, so actors will be formed not with old-fashioned rôles which have been established by several generations of famous stars, but will have to use their intelligence in portraying the verities of everyday life.

The actor will no longer "speak his lines" in the classic sense; he will say them naturally, a thing which is just as difficult to learn. What is at present called the art of "speaking one's lines" consists merely in giving the student an exaggerated articulation, fabricating for him a voice, a special organ entirely different from the one he possesses in reality. For sixty years all actors have uniformly spoken through their noses simply because that method of articulation is necessary in order that they may be heard in our vast auditoriums, which have moreover bad acoustics. All characters to-day make their gestures and express themselves technically in the same fashion, be they old or young, ill or well. All those actors who "speak well" object to those infinitely numerous shadings which establish a character and give him a more intense life. Their pronunciation is entirely different from the current one of to-day. In most of our theatres our players do not speak, they shout, and these unhappy individuals acquire this habit to such an extent that, even when they are in the street, they are picked out as actors in a group of ten talkers.

A like transformation must take place in other fields of dramatic art. The stage-setting must be reduced to limits that will be in conformity with the surroundings of contemporary life, and characters must move about in a more realistic element. They must not be concerned with the necessity of "making tableaux." The spectator will enjoy in an intimate play the simple and appropriate gestures of a modern man, living our everyday life. Then too, the actor must modify his movements; he will not constantly come out of the picture to pose before the audience, he will move about among the furniture and accessories, and his acting will be amplified by a thousand and one nuances and by a thousand and one details which have become indispensable in moulding a character logically. Purely mechanical movements, vocal effects, irrational and superfluous gestures will be banished. Dramatic action will be simplified by a return to reality and natural gestures. The old stagy attitudes will be replaced by effects produced only by the voice. Feelings will be expressed by familiar and real accessories; a pencil turned around, a cup overturned, will be as significant and have an effect as intense on the mind of the spectator as the grandiloquent exaggerations of the romantic drama.

Is it necessary to note that this apparent revolution is nothing but a return to the great traditions and that the most famous actors of the French stage got their finest effects from simple means? Has not Salvini moved us deeply by his sobriety of gesture? And has not Got, dean of our actors, established in a long series of really modern creations, the power of an art that is admirable because of its simplicity? Has not Mounet-Sully obtained in his Hamlet the most artistic creation of his career with contrasts that were simple and almost trivial? Did not Molière himself, in two or three instances, take care to affirm the necessity of "acting as one speaks"? And did not his Mascarille poke fun at the *comédiens* who cannot or will not emphasize "the high spots"?

One might almost say, paradoxical though it may seem, that "in the actor the profession is the enemy of art"; that abnormally developed and ubiquitous professionalism stifles all personality by its cleverness, and dominates the noblest quality of the dramatic performer, emotion, a sensibility raised to the nth power, which pervades the true artist. In acting as in all the arts, sincerity, passion, conviction, that peculiar fever which shakes the soul of the interpreter, are his most precious gifts. But dramatic teaching, as it is now applied, kills these emotional qualities and reduces all temperaments to one level. Our greatest stars were but mediocre pupils, precisely because the artist in them rebelled against traditions and narrow exclusive teachings. How many of the ten celebrated actors in Paris were noticed at the public competitions of the *Conservatoire*. Stendhal, who was once asked if he ever saw a perfect rendering of a play, answered, "Yes, once, in Italy by mediocre players in a barn." He evidently meant that the ensemble which these obscure actors displayed was perfect. And he was surely right, for is not ensemble on the stage the most exquisite joy that can be imagined? We must admit that this treat is almost impossible to-day, even at the Comédie-Française, which has in some respects the most remarkable troupe of actors in Europe.

The Comédie-Française finds itself in the same situation to-day as the other theatres of Paris, where the star system is doing such injury to dramatic art and to the box-office receipts as well. In all theatres, everything gravitates about one or two artists of the first order. But in such a state of things, what becomes of the equilibrium and harmony of a dramatic work from a strictly artistic point of view? Actors are concerned only with their own parts, and will go to the extreme of throwing the play entirely out of equilibrium in order to make their parts stand out.

A model ensemble troupe would consist of some thirty players of equal ability, of ordinary talent, of simple personality, who would yield always and in spite of every other consideration to that fundamental law of ensemble.

[Then follows the long letter that Antoine had written to Sarcey in praise of the ensemble qualities of the Meininger.]

There is one other problem that cannot be passed over in silence, continues Antoine — that of the luxury of the Paris stage. The money spent on tinsel and spangles in our stage-setting might well be put to other uses. But that is not so important as the question of women's gowns. It is not rare to find actresses spending 12,000 to 15,000 francs in clothes for one play alone. And our directors insist upon this. It is impossible for these women to pay for their dresses out of their salaries. There is a moral issue involved here which cannot be ignored. An actress cannot do serious work if she is preoccupied with considerations of this kind. And she seems to think that she must show off her fine raiment in every kind of rôle. It is not rare to find chambermaids dressed like duchesses. Certain plays, it is true, might require robes from our renowned dressmaking establishments; but it seems to me that actresses might well be required to dress in keeping with the characters assigned to them. Is there anything more disgusting than to see a woman hampered in her movements by a brand new gown, and obsessed by fear of spoiling it?

As for the *mise-en-scène*, we have a school of scene painters which holds the first place in Europe. Our masters cannot be rivalled in the making of back-drops. And yet in spite of that, what a profound impression the English and German stage-settings have made upon some of us who have seen them! We feel that they are much superior artistically to the most perfect and sumptuous decorations on our own stage. It is astonishing that Paris, whose dramatic productions are in demand all over the world, whose actors are classed among the first, and whose theatrical art in general has always enjoyed an indisputable superiority, should be so far behind from the purely material point of view. Now we must face the situation frankly, however humbling it may be to our pride, and admit that in scenic illusion we are still in our infancy. None of our theatres, not even the Châtelet which is our best-equipped playhouse mechanically, can present a work in ten tableaux, like *Hamlet* for instance, without long waits. We are still using ridiculous back-drops which have no atmosphere or depth, on which we do not hesitate to paint furniture or even a staircase within three metres of the footlights, which in a crude light can make no pretense at scenic illusions.

Now we propose to improve existing conditions in Paris with the new stage of the Théâtre-Libre. Innovations will be made for the modern plays of the realistic school of drama. We must realize, for instance, the wonderful possibilities of the effects produced by real wood-panels instead of canvas. We must have settings that shall be in conformity with the modern apartments in which we of to-day live. In open-air tableaux we must experiment with suppressing the wing entirely. We must eliminate all false framework which tends to distort the picture. Some of our artists believe that by using certain processes, painted scenery will take on an entirely new relief and give an impression of natural life. In fact the field is vast, but all our plans are possible with the large stage which we hope to have, a stage that will be equipped with all the facilities now made possible by the new discoveries in electricity and in hydraulics. The Théâtre-Libre stage will have considerable depth, and a width of twelve metres, which can be diminished in conformity with the character of the tableaux.

The new theatre will be built on a lot facing the boulevards, not far from the Opéra, and will be called the Théâtre-Libre. The auditorium, constructed in accordance with the blueprints reproduced herewith, will contain 900 seats. It will be of such dimensions that the actor using a natural tone of voice will be easily heard everywhere. The cost of the seats will be about one half of that in vogue in our regular theatres. The best features of foreign theatres which have been already described, will be borrowed for our playhouse. The stage will be provided with mechanical contrivances and a lighting system hitherto unknown in Paris, and will make possible the presentation without entr'actes of dramatic conceptions of any nature.

The Théâtre-Libre company will consist of thirty-five actors and actresses. They will receive an annual salary and will share in the profits. They will play all parts assigned to them by the management. The chief rôles will be taken by different actors in turn during the run of a single play. Their names will never be advertised on the public bills, which will announce simply the name of the play, the time of the performance and its author. Plays will be changed every two weeks, regardless of failure or success. To delay for a successful play would be to reduce production. There will be sixteen performances each season. The first performance of each ·play will be closed to the public, and devoted solely to the press, invited guests, and honorary members of the Théâtre-Libre. The latter will enjoy the possession of a seat for sixteen performances in return for their subscriptions. In case of difficulties with the censorship, the Théâtre-Libre will resume its old functions and will give private performances of the disputed play. In all other respects the Théâtre-Libre will resemble the ordinary theatre. The choice of plays, setting, and distribution of parts will remain under the exclusive direction of M. Antoine.

Then follows a chapter on financing the project. Antoine goes into minute details of budget and probable profits. The actors were to share in twenty-five per cent of the returns, which were estimated at 182,000 francs for the first year. The director, however, was not to be a profit-sharer.

What a dream! What a dreamer! The detailed plan might well serve an idealist manager to-day. All these innovations are not original with Antoine. Zola, Becque, Strindberg, and the Meininger contributed ideas. But Antoine was the first to marshal them into concrete, detailed form. A dramatic Moses, Antoine never saw this promised stageland. Since he dreamed his beautiful dream, two Joshuas, Stanislavski and Copeau, have come nearest to realizing it.

CHAPTER VIII

CENSORS AND SPONSORS
(1890–1891)

THE season of 1890–1891 opened with a very encouraging letter from Larroumet, man of letters, critic, and then Director of Fine Arts in the Ministry of Public Instruction, by which the Théâtre-Libre was allotted 500 francs in the form of four subscriptions. Meanwhile the death of one Brasseur halted plans for a series of public performances of Théâtre-Libre plays. It was now found necessary to give each play three times — one public rehearsal and two subscription performances. The new season was inaugurated with Fèvre's *L'Honneur*, a dramatization of the author's novel, a crude and brutal picture of bourgeois life in the manner of *La Sérénade*. *Monsieur Bute* by Maurice Biollay is an interesting study of an executioner whose mind has been affected by the loss of his position. He kills his servant and drinks her blood. The exposition is ingenious. M. Bute relates his experiences to a newspaper reporter and incidentally to the audience. The ending, however, is overdone and smacks of the slaughter-house. Scholl's *Amant de sa femme* was the best-liked play of the evening. Because of its clever dialogue and licentious innuendos, it still holds the boards in the repertory of the Grand Guignol.

About this time a merry war had arisen over the revival of Becque's *Parisienne* at the Comédie-Française. Never had a play a more stormy career. Originally

refused at the Comédie-Française, later played at the
Renaissance, then at the Comédie-Française again and
at the Vaudeville, it is to-day in the repertory of the
Comédie-Française. It symbolized better than any other
work the crusade for the new school of drama. Antoine
jumped into the fray at an early stage and insisted that
its failure was due to the inability of the actors to understand the author.

In one of his periodical letters to Sarcey, Antoine set
forth what he believed to be the causes of the failure of
La Parisienne at the Comédie-Française:

Are you not struck by this coincidence, three plays, *La Parisienne*, *Grand'mère*, *Le Maître*, all coming from the same camp, conceived in the same spirit of renovation which torments the new
school, failing all three, in three different theatres, none, according
to general opinion, receiving adequate interpretation at the hands
of actors who, nevertheless, belong for the most part to the élite of
the Paris stage? How explain this triple coincidence, and is it not
interesting to seek the causes of it? You will note of course that I
do not permit myself to indulge in literary appreciations: that is
not my business. I speak simply as an actor and as a producer.
Well, I think that there is an important technical question to be
elucidated which ought to interest all the authors of to-morrow, and
perhaps also intelligent and thoughtful players who are concerned
about their art and about the present dramatic movement. *Grand'-
mère* was a failure, *Le Maître* was a failure, and *La Parisienne* is,
you say, a failure.

The press was in general agreed in considering the interpretation
of the three plays mediocre. . . . Well, the very simple explanation
of the triple failure in which players, excellent as a rule, were judged
mediocre one evening, and for that time alone, is that none of these
three works was staged and acted in the right way.

The fact is that this new (or renewed) drama requires new interpreters. Works of observation (or so-called works of observation, if
you will) ought not to be played as other plays of the repertory or
as fanciful comedies are presented. To get under the skin of these
modern characters, one must throw overboard all the old conventions. A realistic play must be played realistically, just as a classic

play must be declaimed, since the character is, more often than not, nothing but an abstraction, a synthesis, without material life. The characters of *La Parisienne* or of *Grand'mère* are people like ourselves, living, not in immense halls of cathedral-like dimensions, but in interiors like ours, at their firesides, under the lamp, around a table, and not at all, as in the old repertory, in front of the prompter's box. They have voices like ours, their language is that of our daily lives, with its elisions, its familiar terms, and not the rhetorical and noble style of our classics.

When Mlle. Reichenberg attacks the first scene in *La Parisienne* in her actress tone of voice, and when M. Prud'hon answers her in the timbre of Molière's Dorante, they are immediately reciting Becque's prose out of tune, and they did it the other evening for three hours without tiring each other. The characteristic element of this new drama is, you will agree, the unconsciousness of the characters, just as we ourselves do stupid and criminal things without being conscious of them. Most of our players, as soon as they appear on the scene, are prone to substitute their own personality for the fellow whom they should make live; instead of their entering into the created character, it is their own character which enters into that of the playwright. And so the other evening we had Mlle. Reichenberg and not Clotilde, MM. Prud'hon, Le Bargy, and de Feraudy, but not Becque's men.

And that salon! Did you ever see in the home of a Paris bourgeois a salon like it? Is that the dwelling of a chief clerk? A dwelling without the slightest suggestion of a corner where one may feel as one does in the house of any of us, that there is somewhere a preferred spot for a chat, an armchair where one may loaf, after the day's work is done?

I know your objection, the setting is secondary. Yes, perhaps, in the classic play, all right. But why not use a realistic setting, since it can be done with care and moderation and would in no way injure the play? In modern works written in a vein of realism and naturalism, where the theory of environment and the influence of exterior things have become so important, is not the setting the indispensable complement of the work? Should it not assume on the stage the same importance as description in a novel? Is it not a sort of exposition of the subject? We shall certainly never portray absolutely true conditions, since on the stage — no one one can deny it — there are a minimum number of conventions that must be observed. But why not make an effort to reduce that minimum?

The size of the stage or of the playhouse is of little importance. If the frame is too large, why not push forward the space where the action takes place and restrict it? And as for diction, is it not a well-known fact that the acoustics of the hall of the Comédie-Française are excellent? Most of the other theatres, half as small, are less favored. Here is another reason, in any case, for not using those immense settings, where, when it is a question of intimate plays, the voice is lost. . . . What do you expect will become of a play that is filled with life and movement if it is placed in a falsified atmosphere?

The movement of the actors is to my mind as misunderstood as the setting. The goings and comings of the players are not regulated according to the text or in accordance with the sense of the scene, but according to the comfort or the caprice of the individual actor who plays each one for himself, without regard for the others. And those footlights hypnotize them; everyone tries to project himself into the audience as far as possible. I have been told of a theatre where, in the time when gas was used, the actors all burned the bottoms of their trousers at the open gas jets.

Mlle. Reichenberg, the other day, recited her monologues standing as she embroidered, as good housewives knit at the doorstep. Not once did Clotilde and Lafont address each other frankly. In real life, after a couple of sentences so spoken, you would say to your interlocutor, "Look me in the eye, will you, I'm talking to *you!*" and you would be justified. The truth is that for this new drama we shall have to get new interpreters. That is an elementary truth which I repeat everywhere again and again. . . .

I beg of you, turn your attention to these things, and observe. You will be struck with the profound difference that is beginning to manifest itself between the works with modern tendencies and the actors who play in them. There is an important point involved there, and a curious phase of the contemporary movement in the drama. I myself am extremely happy, because an evolution is in process. I should never have dreamed of writing all this, were it not for the fact that it has become a sort of sport to "down," kindly, it is true, but still to "down" the Théâtre-Libre, every time that a play which has come from it seeks adventures elsewhere. Make no mistake about it, we are going to collect still more failures and get whacked for our pains, but we have started something. There is a lot of excavating to be done, and you know that the public is already interested. They said at the beginning that our modest theatre was a passing fad, and that it would disappear one fine evening just as suddenly as it had appeared. Now you know that our public is getting larger each year, and that consequently our field is becoming wider and wider. I have the firm hope that the public will eventually come to the new ideas, but, confound it, we mustn't get excited about it and naïvely imagine that we have conquered at one fell swoop literary success, big box-office receipts, and the admiration of the crowds. Many plays will appear on the billboards before that time, and we are just beginning to grope our way. For the present we must be satisfied with looking back and measuring the ground gained during the past five or six years.

During the fall of the year 1890, the Théâtre-Libre was the subject of hot debates in the Senate and in the Chamber of Deputies, which for weeks filled the columns of the press. The agitation was precipitated by the objections on the part of certain deputies to the action of Larroumet in subscribing to the Théâtre-Libre and in encouraging it officially. The performance of *La Fille Élisa*, a dramatization by Ajalbert of Edmond de Goncourt's novel, added fuel to the flames. Songs and skits appeared, not only in the Paris papers, but in those of the provinces, and the Théâtre-Libre and its plays became a national topic of conversation. First, a measure was introduced in the Senate which threatened to cut from the budget the 500 francs offered by Larroumet, on the ground that the plays of the Théâtre-Libre were not only immoral but unpatriotic, the attack being based on *Les Chapons*, the play that preceded the grant of 500 francs, and *L'Honneur*, the play that immediately followed it. Larroumet defended his action on the ground that the 500 francs did not constitute a subsidy; it was a subscription through which the government could keep watch on what the Théâtre-Libre was doing. He had written his letter of congratulation to Antoine because of the quality of the average Théâtre-Libre play, which he deemed worthy of official recognition by the government. It was important that the state should make known to Antoine the interest that it felt in his work. Léon Bourgeois, then Minister of Public Instructon, came to the defence of Larroumet and reminded his colleagues that the plays were performed behind closed doors, and that, although certain ones could not be defended, the Théâtre-Libre was rendering an important service for dramatic art in France. And here the incident closed. It is interesting to note in passing that one of the most fiery champions of the Théâtre-Libre in the Chamber was the recent President of France, Millerand.

In January of the same year, the director of the Porte Saint-Martin invited Antoine to give there a series of public performances because of a hiatus caused by a sudden departure of Sarah Bernhardt. *La Fille Élisa* was in the repertory, but the censor refused to allow it to be presented. This time the positions were reversed, and Bourgeois was forced to defend the government's action against the Théâtre-Libre. Millerand, then Deputy from the Seine, made a brilliant defence of *La Fille Élisa*, showing that moralists and critics were unanimous in condemning the attitude of the government. They contended that *La Fille Élisa* was not only not immoral but was austere in spirit and sincere in its pleas. Millerand insisted that the government was placing itself in a ridiculous position, as *La Fille Élisa* was far more moral than the lascivious and licentious boulevard plays which were not disturbed. He urged that the censor should suggest certain cuts, as it had done with other plays. Bourgeois replied by quoting Dumas to the effect that the censor at all times has been as unpopular as the proverbial mother-in-law, that he disliked the job of censoring, but that he was bound to carry out the law as an officer of the government. To suggest cuts in *La Fille Élisa* would be tantamount to collaborating with the author, and he had no intention or desire to do that. Furthermore, he pointed out that even Goncourt himself had realized that no government would sanction the production of a play in which its attitude toward prostitution was so severely criticized. This was indeed a curious situation in which the government defended and attacked the Théâtre-Libre in the same month.

The question of censorship was a burning one at the time, and the Théâtre-Libre was not the only sufferer. Sardou's *Thermidor* had been recently barred from the stage for political reasons. Antoine made a *beau geste* to Sardou and offered to produce his play, but the author realized that a work of his at the Théâtre-Libre would be a huge joke. The standard-bearer of conventionalism in the camp of the revolutionaries would have set all the wags agog, and so he declined with thanks. Coppée, whose *Pater* had also been interdicted, this time on religious grounds, promised his play to Antoine, but for some reason or other it was never produced at the Théâtre-Libre. Descaves's *Envers du galon*, which appears in some lists of the repertory of the Théâtre-Libre, was never played there. Rehearsals had begun, but Antoine judged it imprudent to give it during the period when Descaves was under fire because of his anti-militaristic novel, *Sous-Offs*. Antoine was considered important enough in the dramatic world to be convoked by the committee on censorship of the Chamber of Deputies, along with Zola, Goncourt, Sardou, Claretie, and others.

La Fille Élisa, whether sincere in purpose or not, cannot be defended on artistic grounds. Like all dramatizations of the Goncourt novels, it is but a series of tableaux. The first act only is dramatic, and as a one-act play *La Fille Élisa* would pass muster. Élisa, the prostitute, is in love with the soldier Tanchon, from whom she has received a beautiful love-letter which she treasures. To him she is a saint, an angel. Unwilling to besmirch this ideal love, she kills him in a burst of violence when he treats her as a prostitute. It was only the first act which brought about the trouble with the censorship. *La Fille Élisa* is not an immoral play; it is a gross spectacle. It does not wound the conscience; it shocks the eyes and ears. The second act takes place in the court room, where the lawyer for the defence pleads for twenty-five minutes. Only an actor of Antoine's calibre could carry off successfully a scene of that type. The third act discloses Élisa in prison, condemned to silence, a barbarous custom which Goncourt was anxious to reform. *La Fille Élisa* as a whole is a thesis against society which permits prostitution and treats its unfortunate victims like animals. But all this social plea is adequately set forth in the novel. The play has no *raison d'être*.

The outcry against *La Fille Élisa* was aggravated by Auguste Linert's *Conte de Noël*, played the same evening. Although styled by the author a mystery play, it is one of the most brutal works presented at the Théâtre-Libre. It is a weird and unsuccessful blend of mysticism and ultra-realism. A work in which an adulterous child is killed and its body thrown to the pigs on Christmas eve, to the sound of Christmas carols, seems to lack every element of the mystery play. It was one of the few works that were hissed at the Théâtre-Libre. Even that hardened audience could not stomach it.

The public performances given at the Porte Saint-Martin in January, 1891, which included *La Mort du duc d'Enghien*, *La Tante Léontine*, and *L'École des veufs*, were extremely well received. Antoine was deeply elated, because most critics had predicted that these particular plays could never hope to succeed with the general public. They were forced to admit that they were wrong in the light of Antoine's figures. He showed that his average receipts were larger than those of the Odéon, Châtelet, Nouveautés, and even the Menus-Plaisirs, where he presented the plays of the Théâtre-Libre. A tour to Brussels in March also helped his impoverished treasury. Antoine was strongly criticized for scattering the efforts of his troupe, yet it would have been impossible to continue his work without the funds obtained by the public performances in and out of Paris.

In April of this same year yet another Théâtre-Libre author found a place in the regular theatre. Porto-Riche's *Amoureuse*, one of the finest plays of contemporary French drama, was played at the Odéon, and Antoine rightly regarded that event as still another victory for the Théâtre-Libre. Porto-Riche had hitherto been writing in a romantic vein, and one critic accused him of forsaking romanticism for Antoinism.

With Ibsen's *Wild Duck*, the battle veered in another direction. Ibsen had displaced Zola as the inspiration of the revolutionists throughout Europe. *Ghosts* had been the favorite play of the ultra-realist schools. With the *Wild Duck*, Ibsen began a new manner, which in turn influenced the drama of Europe. It was a courageous move on the part of Antoine to produce this most obscure of Ibsen's plays after the failure of the realistic *Ghosts*. "Just as I was the first to open my doors wide to the naturalist drama," said Antoine, "so shall I open them wide also to symbolist drama, provided it is drama."

The *Wild Duck* fell completely flat, flatter than *Ghosts*. Sarcey attacked it most savagely, and Doumic said that it required a violent effort of the French mind to comprehend it. Lemaître, however, ridiculed his colleagues, although he admitted that the *Wild Duck* needed close concentration to be understood. He quoted from one of the translators, Amand Ephraïm, "Isn't it curious that three hundred years after Shakespeare, and one hundred years after Goethe, we pretend in France not to understand an author because he takes as a term of comparison in a tragedy a bird which is not consecrated by Greek mythology?" Antoine was among the very first of the moderns in France to break down this pose, in reality a prejudice against foreign dramatists. To-day, thanks to Antoine and to the directors who have been influenced by him, France is just as hospitable to foreign plays as any country in the world, with the possible exception of the United States, which, having as yet little drama of its own, eagerly accepts new plays from all lands, be they good, bad, or indifferent.

Although he had presented the *Wild Duck* in the face of much adverse comment, Antoine never allowed his admiration for symbolic drama to run away with his good judgment. In spite of repeated urgings, he was never sufficiently convinced as to the value of Maeterlinck's drama to produce a play of his at the Théâtre-Libre. The thirty years that have elapsed since the days of the

Théâtre-Libre seem to have ratified Antoine's judgment. Ibsen and Hauptmann, each of whom was played twice at the Théâtre-Libre, have long since outdistanced Maeterlinck. An enthusiast urged that a third play of Ibsen's be presented, but Antoine opposed the idea, saying that it was not the purpose of the Théâtre-Libre to specialize on any one foreign author. Its work was to blaze new trails for other theatres. They now might follow with other plays of Ibsen.

Toward the close of the season of 1890–1891, Pierre Wolff presented his second play, *Leurs Filles*. Unlike Ancey and Jullien, who are infinitely superior to him, Wolff, who began as a writer of *rosse* plays, has become one of the most successful playwrights in France to-day. Always clever and witty, his work has been praised by the critics and repeatedly finds an audience. Entirely lacking in originality, he has learned the trick of sugar-coating the *rosserie* of his Théâtre-Libre days with a sort of sentimental tenderness by means of which his heroines of the underworld never fail to bring tears to the eyes of his public. *Leurs Filles*, in which we are shown how the daughters of harlots follow the trade of their mothers, in spite of convent educations, gives the measure of Wolff's facile, superficial talent. He had previously produced at the Théâtre-Libre a one-act trifle, *Jacques Bouchard*. Antoine, who had been at swords' points with Pierre's uncle, Albert Wolff of the *Figaro*, took a silent part in this play so that he might stare out of countenance the enraged critic, who, to his profound disgust, found his young nephew becoming one of the pillars of the upstart playhouse which was succeeding in spite of him.

In general the season of 1890–1891 was lacking in dis-

It is evident [he wrote in 1887] that the new school has something against it, something very unfortunate. It has produced nothing. M. Zola, always so convincing in his programmes and claims, has not yet written anything for the stage. Another author has likewise produced nothing. M. Henry Céard is a man who is very strong and sure of himself, but we are still waiting for him to burst forth.

This was too much for Céard, who retaliated by taunting Becque with his own infecundity.

For lack of anything else, M. Becque has deigned to bestow upon the Théâtre-Libre his rare and useless protection. He has given advice to M. Antoine, an easier thing than to have given him a play. Assuredly there is some good in the observations of M. Becque. . . . But why doesn't he follow up his advice? In any event, it was without him that the Théâtre-Libre was created, it was without him that it obtained results.

Antoine thus found himself in a delicate position. Zola, as well as Becque, was one of his dramatic gods. Céard was one of the earliest authors of the Théâtre-Libre and had championed it vigorously in the press. But Antoine felt constrained to reply that he regarded Becque as "the real leader and master of the whole youthful movement, a man whom we all consider the renovator of contemporary drama." Venomous though it was, there was some truth in Céard's charge. Throughout the nine years of the existence of the Théâtre-Libre Becque wrote nothing for it or for any other playhouse. This seems hardly credible, but it is true. Here was an audience deeply prejudiced in his favor, here was a director thirsting for a play from the greatest dramatist of the revolutionary movement, yet Becque could not hatch one for them. Unlike Zola, Becque never wavered in his ideals of dramatic art; he could not and would not make compromises.

But if Becque was powerless to write plays for the Théâtre-Libre, he made it clear by his articles in the press that he regarded it as a mighty agent in carrying on the battle for the revolutionary drama. Like Antoine and so many others, he too disliked the term naturalist in describing the new dramatic movement and always avoided it. Soon after the opening of the Théâtre-Libre, he wrote:

Here we have a director with a very fine perception of all things dramatic, authors who are convinced that they are moving in the right direction, a company filled with ardor, which possesses two inestimable qualities, simplicity and naturalness. From the very first moment that that artistic house was opened, all men of letters flocked to it, and there was no dramatic life last winter outside of that theatre.

On another occasion he wrote:

We are tired. We want something new. Antoine has come and here it is, and it cannot be said too often that he has rendered a tremendous service to dramatic art with his admirable work. . . . His Théâtre-Libre has been a sort of dramatic nursery where so many talented authors have taken their first step, cut their first teeth, and done something more besides.

And, still later:

Among the services that Antoine has rendered to dramatic art, there is one which has not been noticed heretofore. He has delivered us from charlatans. . . . Forward, my boys! Don't complain, it is completely useless to do that. And above all, don't get discouraged; you will regret it later. You are in the field, and the field is free; pass right on over our bodies.

Toward the close of his life, Becque wrote: "The whole dramatic movement of the past ten years has been created by Antoine. All dramatists of to-day and yesterday have been introduced to the public by Antoine. If Ibsen is famous with us, if Dumas has learned the joy of knowing and admiring his great Norwegian contemporary, it is to Antoine that he owes it."

At a banquet given in his honor after his resignation from the Théâtre-Libre, Antoine said of both Zola and Becque: "I wish to greet in your presence, since the occasion has presented itself to me, two masters, Émile Zola and Henry Becque, to whom I owe all my convictions and all the inspiration which has guided my way. Formerly I admired them passionately at a distance, and it will be the honor of my career that they have been willing to count me their friend."

CHAPTER IX

CUREL AND BRIEUX
(1891–1892)

TO INAUGURATE the season of 1891–1892, Balzac's *Père Goriot* appeared in dramatic form. When asked why he had hazarded so perilous an undertaking, Antoine answered:

> It is indeed rather adventurous and we are in perhaps for a good-sized fizzle. But the reputation of the Théâtre-Libre is built upon failures of this kind. What has captivated me is that there is something new at the bottom of this venture. It has never been done, and then it is possible that in the present dramatic mess, the arrival on the stage of the great figures of the *Comédie humaine* may help to reveal some of the unknown elements of the drama of the future. So much the worse for us if we fail, but our duty is to seek out new things. Marching as scouts, at the risk of falling from time to time in the underbrush, we prevent those who come after us from breaking their necks. The work of the Théâtre-Libre will, I think, bring results, not so much through the plays produced as by currents that they may determine.

This, before the presentation. After the gloomy failure he wrote, "My poor *Père Goriot* did not turn out as I had hoped, and yet I swear that never was work of Balzac executed with more conscience or piety."

There appeared about this time the first note of despair in Antoine's words. Much time and money had been spent on what he hoped would be a brilliant success. But the great difficulty was that Tabarant, the dramatizer of Balzac's novel, was even weaker than the average.

Salandri's *Rançon* did not help matters. Salandri never developed beyond a third-rate Becque. Marcel Prevost's *Abbé Pierre*, in which a mother confesses her sin to her son, a priest, was violently criticized for its lack of good taste. The high-water mark of the *rosserie* of the Théâtre-Libre was reached in Ancey's *Dupe*, his fourth and last play there. *La Dupe* has been often cited by critics as a typical play of the Théâtre-Libre. That it was typical of the ultra-realist group of playwrights identified with the Théâtre-Libre is true, but to say that it was representative of the whole Théâtre-Libre movement is gross exaggeration. Ancey had a natural tendency to brutality of language and situation which he intensified at the Théâtre-Libre. His *École des veufs* seemed to have reached the limits of dramatic realism, but *La Dupe* goes one step beyond, in its portrayal of human grossness. In point of construction it has all the old tricks of the conventional play. Its sole originality consists in its extravagant situations and its crude language. Albert, the "hero," goes through his wife's fortune and part of that of her mother. He begs pennies from his wife even after they are separated. He is not only a beggar and wife-beater, but an embezzler to boot; yet Adèle, the dupe, becomes her husband's mistress because she is bound to him by a sexual mania. *La Dupe* transgresses the canons of common decency and shows the ultra-realist movement at its worst. It was the kind of play that turned away from the Théâtre-Libre many who had been previously drawn to it.

Critics were beginning to question the *raison d'être* of the Théâtre-Libre. Ultra-realist plays were being produced everywhere and a pronounced reaction against them was plainly visible. *Hedda Gabler* and the *Doll's House* continued the Ibsen invasion. One of the events of the season which hurt the Théâtre-Libre tremendously was a series of pornographic performances by one Chirac, who was arrested and imprisoned. Either through the malevolence of his enemies or through sheer error, Antoine and the Théâtre-Libre were confused in the public mind with this filthy enterprise.

The situation was saved temporarily by the appearance in February of plays by two unknown authors, François de Curel and Eugène Brieux, both of whom are still close friends of Antoine, and who, with Porto-Riche, may be considered the three greatest French playwrights launched by his theatre. They are the writers who are most truly representative of the Théâtre-Libre. None of them was influenced to any great extent by its dramatic aberrations. All three acknowledge their debt to Antoine and have frequently expressed their gratitude to him publicly. Antoine in turn encouraged and supported them, in and out of the Théâtre-Libre. All three will tell you that they owe more to him than to any man living.

Antoine and Curel both tell the story of the three plays, *L'Amour brodé*, *La Figurante*, and *L'Envers d'une sainte*, sent to Antoine by MM. Watterneau, Weindel, and Curel in 1891. During the summer of that year Antoine picked out these three plays, by supposedly different authors, from among 500 manuscripts submitted for presentation during the season of 1891–1892. Curel had sent the three plays to Antoine with little hope of ever seeing them produced. He had been refused by director after director, and had been told that not even the Théâtre-Libre would accept them because "Antoine was the prisoner of a little clan of naturalists." When it came to the question as to which one of the three plays should be presented, Curel left the matter entirely in Antoine's hands.

I'll put on *L'Envers d'une sainte* [he said to Curel]. It is n't to my interest to do so, because the two other plays would receive a better welcome from my public, and you will find that, with more experience in playwriting, you will produce works which will succeed in the big theatres. *L'Envers d'une sainte*, on the contrary, would for a long time find no other home than with me. Let us play it then. You will at once win a reputation as a writer, a thing not to be despised, but they will say that you are not a dramatic author. Still what difference will that make to you, since you have something in reserve to prove that you are?

Says Curel in the introduction to his complete works:

I cannot speak without emotion of my relations with the Théâtre-Libre. Antoine, in the flower of his youth, gave evidence of a mad activity and passion for the theatre, a passion which devoured him and which kindled all the people about him. The actors of the Théâtre-Libre were not paid, they were recruited from all professions. There were housepainters and dressmakers among them, but they were all sustained by the touching conviction of service to their art and a blind confidence in their leader. When Antoine affirmed that he had discovered a profound genius, each one in his band lavished admiration on the future great man. I have really never felt so sure of myself as when I was in that enthusiastic environment, and I never look backward without a feeling of tenderness and gratitude toward those who were then my interpreters, remarkable because they were so sincere.

Never were rehearsals more laborious than those of *L'Envers d'une sainte*. The rôle of Julie in particular baffled the good-will of everybody. I think that we tried twenty-three or twenty-four Julies before deciding upon Mme. Nancy Vernet. In Antoine's entourage there were certain intimates of his who declared that my play was not actable for the simple reason that it was not a play. And they added by way of refrain, "Antoine, there you are, for the hundredth time, a victim of one of your sudden enthusiasms!" Antoine let them talk and continued his search for the undiscoverable Julie.

Among the many reasons which I have for preserving for Antoine an unfailing gratitude, I place among the first the fact that nothing could ever shake his confidence in my future. Like all comprehensive minds, he would assimilate the ideas of others by mingling with them many ideas of his own. He had frequent enthusiasms because he lavished on mediocre works the fertile fancies of his own imagination. But the gift of improving upon mediocre works cannot but help one to reach finer ones. That is why Antoine's enthusiasms, far from injuring the reputation which he has won for himself, have, on the contrary, contributed to make him wonderfully fecund.

He exercised a prodigious influence over his company of actors; he was an apostle teaching new doctrines, and a master in indicating the way to apply them. His most insignificant judgments were listened to religiously. When he announced the coming of a man of genius, all the faces about him were illuminated with a look of triumph. Thanks to a little act played at the Théâtre-Libre, an author had the sensation for a year of being a great man. As for me, the glorious hours that I have lived in the humble room in the Rue Blanche remain the most beautiful of my literary life. The people whom I met there really deserve the name of artists, a name usurped by so many second-raters. . . . They loved their art with a disinterested passion and played with a heart that gave us interpreters which the highest official theatres were incapable of equalling.

It was the enthusiasm of Antoine which carried off *L'Envers d'une sainte* at the time of its reading at Rue Blanche. He himself was so warm in his appreciation that he covered up the lukewarmness of his band. But he could not do the same the night of the performance, which took place in February, 1892. The audience received *L'Envers d'une sainte* very coldly and even jeeringly. One auditor states that, when the curtain went up for the third act, he was the only person left in the balcony. Antoine had to seize one of his subscribers who was opening and shutting a door in order to drown out the words of the actors, march him down to the box-office, and refund him his subscription money. He himself records that the audience was stupid, stamping whenever it could, but despite all that, the press has made M. de Curel famous. There is no doubt as to the value of the play, everybody is convinced that it is something out of the ordinary. The result is all the more remarkable because it was played rather poorly; it is a kind of drama so new, so psychological, that it is extremely difficult to interpret.

When Antoine spoke of "the press," he meant, of course, the handful of discriminating critics like Lemaître, Faguet, Bauer, Fouquier, and Doumic, who welcomed Curel as an original and powerful young dramatist. To Curel he said: "A fine crowd of idiots my subscribers are. They come to us to be amused, and by Jove, you give them *Bérénice*." Small wonder then that Curel should feel so loyal to Antoine. In spite of his collaborators, his actors, and his audience, Antoine was sure he had discovered a genius and stuck to his guns. And he has so persisted in ramming his belief in Curel down the throats of the French people that they have finally accepted him as the flower of their contemporary drama.

In an address which Curel gave at his reception into the Academy, he said:

That so-called prisoner of the naturalist school, Antoine, has the most independent mind that I have ever known, and when he inscribed the word "free" on the front of his theatre, it was not without reason. The greatest service rendered by the Théâtre-Libre has been to free the modern stage from all schools and from all literary coteries. The day will come when justice will be done to our dramatic epoch and when the originality that resulted from the independence of the Théâtre-Libre will be felt.

In spite of all the alterations that Curel has made in *L'Envers d'une sainte* since its first appearance, it has always remained a promise rather than a fulfillment. Nevertheless, it was a brilliant promise. Like most of Curel's works, it is a minute analytical study of the

primitive instincts of humanity. Julie Renaudin has se-
questered herself in a convent for eighteen years, expi-
ating a crime of attempted murder. She had been in love
with her cousin Henri, who had jilted her, gone to Paris,
and brought back a wife. In a fit of insane jealousy, Julie
pushes the young wife, who is about to become a mother,
into a ravine. This action brings about the premature
birth of Jeanne's child Christine. All the foregoing events
have happened eighteen years before the opening of the
play. Soon after Henri's death, Julie comes home from
her convent and discovers that Henri has been told of
the crime which she thought had been kept from him,
to whom she wished to appear a martyr of love. Julie is
not of the stuff of which saints are made, in spite of her
eighteen years of convent life, and she wreaks vengeance
on Jeanne by persuading her daughter Christine to give
up her fiancé and take the veil. But when she finds that
Henri had exacted on his death-bed a promise from
Christine that she should be kind to his former sweetheart, whom he had wronged, her plan of vengeance becomes unnecessary, and she secures a promise from Christine to give up all thought of going to a convent. Julie
herself returns, instead. But somewhere in the remote
recesses of her soul, Julie has a murderous instinct. Before leaving her home, she crushes to death a little bird
which she happens to find, explaining that death is more
to be desired than imprisonment for life. Thus we see the
other side of a nun rather than that of a saint. Julie was
never a saint.

Although Curel has never been concerned with box-
office receipts and has been little swayed by criticism, favorable or unfavorable, still he has considerably changed

his plays in several instances. *Sauvée des eaux*, later
L'Amour brode, finally appeared as *La Danse devant le
miroir*, almost completely rewritten. *L'Envers d'une
sainte*, originally *L'Ortie*, probably inspired by the lines
"elle a jeté son froc aux orties" (she has cast her veil into
the nettles), spoken of Julie when she leaves her convent,
has been entirely revised in its present form. In the original text as played at the Théâtre-Libre, two characters,
Noémie, an aunt, who is the confidant of Julie, and
Georges, Christine's fiancé, appear, and in the new version
there is added Madame de Frévoir, a former pupil of
Julie, who appears now as Odile and now as Odette.
She is a sort of intruder in the revised version and has
no real place there. She is so unfamiliar to the author
that he forgets her name.

L'Envers d'une sainte has never been revived, to my
knowledge, and in its present state is never likely to be
seen behind the footlights. Clumsy as the original version
is, it is much better than the retouched, strained work
which Curel in his later days of fame has written.
Why must dramatists tinker with the works of their
youth? In the old play Julie is one of those savage ele-
mental creatures of Curel. She may be cruel and in-
human and abnormal, but she rings truer than the pale,
softened Julie of the second version.

L'Envers d'une sainte centres almost entirely on Julie.
The other characters are mere puppets, which are necessary only because they provide material to play upon
Julie's emotions. Julie, like almost all Curel's protagonists, is a passionate, primitive creature with uncon-
trolled and uncontrollable instincts. She has gone to her
convent, not so much through remorse as through self-

chastisement, which carries with it a sort of spectacular martyrdom. Curel is deeply concerned with the selfish instincts in man's motives, and Julie is more a type than a living, breathing human being. His portrayal is intensely analytical but not psychological. He analyzes motives but he does not explain them. He is mainly concerned with ideas, and so the play is rather a dramatic study than drama.

By a singular contradiction [says Curel], my mind, naturally inclined to seek the reason of things, expresses itself easily only in dramatic form. What shall you say of a soul in which the meditative curiosity of a Montaigne is united to the fanciful outpourings of a Musset? . . . Characters present themselves to my imagination passionate and vibrating, but I am tormented with a desire to go back to the causes which make them act, whence it results that in my plays the thought goes hand in hand with the action. A combination fraught with difficulty if I want to conquer my public upon which is imposed the double task of getting interested in my plot and of assimilating my idea. . . . Yes, thought is the worst enemy of a dramatic author, and each time that he brings it into a play without meeting disaster, he accomplishes a miracle.

That miracle was not accomplished in *L'Envers d'une sainte*. It is a play to be read, or acted before a select public. Even Antoine's picked audience would not accept it. But the important point to be borne in mind is that Antoine, with his keen intuition, divined the dramatic thinker in Curel, and despite the woeful failure of *L'Envers d'une sainte*, was soon engrossed in the production of a new play by the same author. Antoine had realized that Curel had struck an original note in contemporary French drama, and was little concerned that he was not primarily a dramatist. He had accepted so many ultra-realist writers because they were trying to reinvigorate French drama, not because they were extremists. They were a sort of *pis aller*, the best that he could get. In Curel, however, he sensed a great dramatic poet. So he gave him a double welcome to the Théâtre-Libre and defended him hotly against almost unanimous opposition.

Curel was not the only French dramatist introduced to France on the night of February 2, 1893. Brieux made himself famous with *Blanchette*, one of the best known of contemporary French plays, now on the repertory of the Comédie-Française. It was warmly received on the night of the first performance, and became one of the most popular plays of Antoine's ambulant repertory. He was always sure of making a hit with *Blanchette*, before no matter what kind of audience, in no matter what country of Europe. Brieux had already produced his *Ménages d'Artistes* at the Théâtre-Libre, but it had passed almost unnoticed, as it deserved. Brieux himself confesses that "it contains scarcely a scene which justified Antoine's production of it." He published it later in his complete works only because he felt "a sort of loyalty in not suppressing it." He goes on to say, "The undying gratitude which I have for Antoine is due precisely to the fact that he played a really bad work of mine."

I was then [says Brieux, writing of his experiences with *Ménages d'Artistes*] a journalist at Rouen, and not only was my name unknown in Paris, but also my person, to such an extent that I could witness the dress rehearsal and first performance of my play right in the middle of the orchestra like a simple spectator. Never did I receive a more severe lesson in dramatic art. All my faults, all my lack of experience were paraded before me and appeared striking. I was part of that collective soul which is created each evening in a theatre audience, and I suddenly became extremely perspicacious. I did not judge myself; I shared the feelings of the audience toward the work presented. . . . That evening I learned many things. I don't mean

to say that I perceived all my clumsiness and understood the reason
for the public's unwillingness to accept my play, or that I deduced
from this the laws of dramatic art. But there certainly penetrated
my cranium, which was tortured with a migraine, dumbfounded,
overwhelmed, lessons, which, of my own accord, I should have been
incapable of formulating, of indicating, or of distinguishing, and
which were received not by my intelligence but by my instinct.
Nothing could have been worth more than that lesson. It is quite
certain that I learned more in the course of a few hours than if I had
burned the midnight oil for years on theoretical studies and on
treatises on dramatic art. And so once more, thanks, Antoine.

Ménages d'Artistes had been dedicated to Antoine, so
was *Blanchette*.

My dear friend [writes Brieux], for ten years I took my manuscripts to all the theatres of Paris. More often than not, they were
not even read. Thanks to you, thanks to the Théâtre-Libre, I can
at last learn my profession of dramatic author, and here is the second
play of mine that you have produced within two years. I take this
occasion to thank you publicly for it.

As it is played now at the Comédie-Française, *Blanchette* follows a third and presumably final ending. In
version number one, Blanchette is a young country girl
educated beyond her station. While marking time, waiting for an appointment in a government school, she turns
her father's wine-shop topsy-turvy with her high-falutin'
ideas. Driven from home by an irate father, she gets discouraged, and like many another heroine of Brieux throws
herself into the Seine. She is rescued, however, and becomes the mistress of the brother of a wealthy boarding-
school friend. Returning home she finds her father's property about to be sold for debts and offers to pay them.
But he will have none of her tainted money, and she
returns to Paris to live the life of a prostitute, crying as
the curtain falls, "Suckers beware!" Brieux evidently con-

siders this ending too *rosse*. In the second version, Blanchette returns chastened in spirit, and persuades her father to accept her money just as the family sits down to table reciting the *Benedicite*. In the last version, the third act is completely changed. Blanchette returns home virtuous, the wine-shop is not in financial danger, and she marries a country bumpkin whom she had refused in her proud days.

None of these third acts is satisfactory. The first two are melodramatic, verbose, and preachy. The third is sugary, or, according to Brieux, "agreeable." Antoine was never satisfied with any of these third acts, and often played Blanchette as a two-act play. Considered as a two-act play, *Blanchette* is as good as anything Brieux has ever written, with the possible exception of *Les Hannetons*. It may seem carping to criticize Brieux's endings in the light of what Molière has done with his last scenes, but then Brieux, in spite of Shaw's encomiums, is not a Molière, he is really more of a Shaw. He is a missionary, a social reformer, but not a great dramatist. This he is himself the first to admit. "The steaks that I have enjoyed in this world are justified by the good that I have done," he once confided in a reminiscent mood. Brieux admits that *Blanchette* ends with the fall of the curtain at the close of the second act. It was only to satisfy the sentimental curiosity of the public that the author was forced to tell what eventually became of his heroine.

It was Sarcey who first showed Brieux the error of his "naturalist" ways, by insisting that the first ending was but a convention of the *théâtre rosse*, and that Brieux wrote it only because he was afraid of being ridiculed by

the so-called reformers. Brieux tells us how he was led
astray.

> I wrote *Blanchette* at Rouen in 1890. At that time the Théâtre-
> Libre was in its heroic period. Its champions went out of their way
> to protest against the romantic, fanciful, conventional, and senti-
> mental drama. And they went out of their way with a vengeance.
> On the first nights of the Théâtre-Libre I escaped from Rouen when-
> ever I could, and after the performance I would accompany Antoine
> and his friends to some café. There we would comment upon the
> events of the evening. Whenever the plays had brought forth vocif-
> erous comments from the audience, Antoine would enjoy the rebel-
> lion of the spectators. "My, did n't they drool," he would say, his
> eyes shining with joy. And we almost believed him when with a
> word of optimism which finally deceived even himself, he would
> conclude, "Well, a fine evening for the Théâtre-Libre." We looked at
> him with respect, as one looks upon someone who possesses a point
> of resemblance with Providence whose designs are impenetrable.
>
> My turn of mind naturally led me away from dogmatic pessimism
> and violence of language. But in my province I was nevertheless a
> little intoxicated by that rarified atmosphere which I used to go to
> breathe as often as possible at the Théâtre-Libre, and in writing the
> third act of Blanchette, I wanted to show those wolves, whose haught-
> iness and talent imposed itself upon me, that I too had teeth.

And thus it was that Brieux became a "naturalist." But
he ceased to be a "naturalist" when he rewrote the third
act of *Blanchette*, and his later plays belong rather to the
field of sociology than to that of the drama. One exception must be made in the case of his *Hannetons*, a *rosse*
satire on the *ménage à trois*, which reminds one very
strongly of *La Tante Léontine*, a play that seems to have
made a great impression on Brieux's mind. *Les Hannetons*
is Brieux's best play, and so by the irony of fate, posterity will probably classify him as a dramatist of *rosse*
plays in spite of himself.

It was in the spring of this year, 1892, that Porel, who
had followed more closely than any other director of

Paris the work of the Théâtre-Libre, resigned. Antoine
was urged by his friends to present himself as a candidate
for the directorship of the Odéon, but he felt that the
time was not ripe, and that he still had things to do at
the Théâtre-Libre.

Gramont's *Simone*, played in April, 1892, was one of
the most literary works of the Théâtre-Libre. Epigram-
matic and brilliant in spots, it is a forerunner of the
psychoanalytic play of to-day, a physiological study of
marital relations with a strong medical flavor to it, which
leaves nothing unsaid on the intimate conjugal relations
of the protagonists. One critic characterized it as a dramatic counterpart to Balzac's *Physiologie du mariage*.

With the close of the year 1891–1892 a rather paradoxical situation existed with regard to the Théâtre-Libre.
The season had not been a brilliant one and Antoine was
much discouraged as to the future. Young authors who
had been tried out at the Théâtre-Libre were being accepted elsewhere and all the best actors were being enticed
away. Yet, had the Théâtre-Libre not been regarded as
a model in things dramatic, nothing of the kind would
have happened. Porto-Riche and Jullien had been accepted at the Odéon, Hennique and Pierre Wolff at the
Gymnase, Méténier at the Variétés, and Lavedan at the
Vaudeville. The actors, Grand, Mayer, Janvier, and Luce
Colas were taken by the legitimate theatres. Then too,
the Théâtre-Libre was being used as a sort of laboratory
by the students of the *Conservatoire* and by young actors
of larger theatres as a place to serve their apprenticeship. Provincial and foreign tours helped to pay off increasing debts, but the meticulous artist in Antoine
forced him to maintain a ruinously expensive workshop

where special scenery for each play was made, in spite of the fact that his contract with the Menus-Plaisirs gave him the right to use the scenery of that theatre.

Each year, as the importance of the Théâtre-Libre increased, its enemies increased in proportion. Bauer, having won the suit instigated by Antoine for defamation of character, was willing to call quits, but Antoine's former adherents, Céard and Jullien, had fallen upon him most savagely for his unwillingness to listen to their advice. In spite of the opposition to the tours, which in the minds of the critics were sapping the energies of his troupe, Antoine started the season of 1892–1893 with a financially successful trip. In Marseilles he met a group of young men who had founded a Théâtre-Libre there. Among them was Émile Fabre, now director of the Comédie-Française, whose *Argent* had been accepted for the Paris Théâtre-Libre, and Auguste Rondel, who has recently presented to the Comédie-Française a magnificent library of dramatic literature which will be of inestimable value to students of drama in Paris.

CHAPTER X

THE HIGH–WATER MARK
(1892–1893)

THE first important dramatic event of the season of
1892–1893 was the presentation of Curel's second
play, *Les Fossiles*. It is now in the repertory of the Comédie-Française and, bearing out the promise of *L'Envers
d'une sainte*, definitely established Curel's reputation as
a dramatist. It opened for him the doors of the Comédie-Française for his next play but one, *L'Amour brode*.
In October of the previous year, Henri de Bornier had
shown how the Théâtre-Libre had planted its flag upon
the principal theatres of Paris. "The authors of the
Théâtre-Libre will before long be the masters of the
stage," he predicted. "To-morrow perhaps some audacious soldier of M. Antoine will demolish with melenite
shells our fortifications of the Comédie-Française."
Within a year his prophecy had come true. The last line
of defence of the conservatives had been broken down
by the onslaughts of Curel and Brieux.

Les Fossiles are the nobles whose last representatives
on earth must leave the same impression of grandeur as
the gigantic fossils which are the relics of remote ages.
Robert de Chantemelle, the dying son of a decadent
family leaves a son born in incest. But the traditions of
his house must be carried on even though tarnished.
The first two acts and part of the third are intensely

dramatic and are made of such stuff as went into the
Greek tragedies. Euripides has said that wars between
brothers are terrible. Then wars between father and son
are doubly terrible. The following is an example of the
power of the dialogue of *Les Fossiles*.

DUKE (*father of Robert*).—I shall keep the child in spite of you,
in spite of his mother.
ROBERT. — The child is mine.
DUKE. — Ours.
ROBERT. — Mine.
DUKE (*in a terrible voice*). — Ours!
CLAIRE (*Robert's sister, in terror*). — Papa! Papa! think what
you are saying!
DUKE (*pushing Claire away*). You, get out! . . . Get out! . . . this
is between him and me!
CLAIRE. — Please!
DUKE.—Get out! (*He takes Claire by the shoulders and pushes her
out. She can be seen standing behind the door which is not closed.
Rushes up to Robert in an outburst of terrible passion.*) — Ours! I had
relations with the mother at Chantemelle before you. I committed
the crime of making you marry her, in order to perpetuate the name
which was dying out. And I shall not let you snatch away from us
to turn over to unworthy hands the child so dearly bought! He
belongs to the family, I forbid you to touch him. That's all I have
to say. (*Suddenly calm and haughty.*) Now if you want me to die, I
am ready!
ROBERT (*looks long and fixedly at the duke, then he goes tottering
toward the door. As he is about to go out, he collects the little strength
left to him, straightens himself up and says*): One of us two must die!
(*He goes out tottering; at the door, he falls into the arms of Claire who
is waiting for him.*)

It is of course Robert who dies. The fourth act is a
philosophical epilogue where Robert's will is read. He
leaves to his criminally born son the task of perpetuating
the traditions of the Chantemelle family.

The third act is pure poetry. Yet poetry is precisely
what most of the realist plays of the Théâtre-Libre

lacked. By injecting poetry into his work Curel raised it above the level of the banal, *rosse* play and made it worthy of a place in French literature. Robert de Chantemelle is a poet and a dreamer into whose character the author has put some of his own doubts and hesitations. Although an aristocrat, Robert is not blind to the benefits of democracy. Like Curel himself, he is too much imbued with the spirit of Montaigne to have profound convictions.

Claire has just said to her brother, "You certainly prefer the forests to the sea." To which he replies:

I love them both, but not with the same heart. In me the aristocrat worships those lofty trees which are as old as ourselves, whose branches protect a whole people of shrubs. Are we not brothers of the oaks and gigantic beeches? It is impossible for me to walk among them without sharing their arrogance. I soar above the dwarf saplings, I take for myself all the light, and scatter disdainfully beechnuts and acorns to the famished dwellers of the moors. Here, in the presence of the sea, a different man is awakened in me. The waves, one just like the other, come in battalions dashing upon the shore, all equally glittering in the sunshine, all equally smooth in calm weather, all equally rough in the storm. Then I say to myself that here is a picture of humanity totally different from that of the woods. The uniformity of those waves, each bearing its share of the weight of ships, and on which the gulls alight where they will, disturbs a little my forest instincts. I ask myself whether man could not advance in unison like the waves, which, without clashing, rush together to the shore. But immediately a fear assails me. I doubt whether humanity—provided a perfect levelling of it can ever be realized —will continue to mount toward its mysterious destinies like the legions of waves which rise in a mass when attacked from on high. My choice hesitates at the memory of those gigantic trees which are marvels if they are allowed to strangle everything that grows about them. So you must pity me, torn as I am between the woodman and the sailor, the man of the forest and the man of the sea. . . . I am a *déclassé!* My century claims me through my brain, the past holds my heart! No matter where I go, it is exile for one half of me.

Curel has often been criticized because he does not solve his problems. In *Les Fossiles* his problem is a struggle between aristocracy and democracy; in later plays it is between socialism and capitalism, science and religion, faith and speculation, patriotism and egotism, love and sexual attraction. He always leaves the question in the air and never takes sides. Most of his plays might well end with the famous query of Montaigne, "Que sais-je?" As well criticize Hamlet for his velleity. Curel is a playwright of ideas. The characters which clothe his ideas in dramatic form are often supermen. We cannot visualize them in the humdrum occupations of everyday life. They are given to introspective criticism of their own acts, but it is not always clear why they should have committed these acts. They are at times capable of action and forceful action, even of murder. Curel never seems to consider man in relation to society, he is mainly interested in the influence of man's deeds upon himself. His plays then are conflicts of ideas rather than conflicts of personalities. The author does not arouse our emotions by situations which have every possibility of dramatic development; he uses his situations as a basis for long ethical and philosophical discussions. Dramatic action is to him a means to an end, and that is why he has never been a popular playwright. It is to the great glory of Antoine that his iconoclastic theatre introduced this iconoclastic author to French audiences.

Although most of Curel's plays have failed on the stage, they are likely to live longer as literature than some of the more popular productions of his contemporaries. He may have refused to abide by the accepted laws of dramatic technique, yet he was exceedingly exacting with himself in the matter of style. Every word, every phrase, is carefully polished; his style is as aristocratic as the man himself. His descriptions of forest and sea in *Les Fossiles* are eloquent of his own love of nature, and are among the most beautiful in modern French literature. His works stand out as the loftiest and most noble expression of contemporary French drama.

Sarcey grudgingly praised the literary qualities of *Les Fossiles*, and let it be said to his credit, saw more promise in the unconventional Curel than in the conventional playwright Hervieu. Lemaître, who found *L'Envers d'une sainte* not unworthy of an Ibsen, was reminded by *Les Fossiles* of the great Corneille. Curel had first sent *Les Fossiles* to Claretie of the Comédie-Française, but the latter refused it on the ground that it was not fit for the ears of respectable people. And yet in 1897, after Curel had made his reputation, the Comédie-Française took the play which the Théâtre-Libre had taught it to respect. "It is evident," says Curel, "that the 'respectable people' of 1892 had more sensitive ears than those of 1897 to whom I offered a considerably modified play, modified but not toned down."

The interpretation of *Les Fossiles* at the Théâtre-Libre was evidently not up to the play itself, and the acting and setting were severely criticized by the press. Sarcey and Lemaître were particularly harsh with Antoine on that score. Right here we can see the beginning of the end of Antoine's long struggle. The Théâtre-Libre was becoming demoralized by constant losses of actors and by careless productions of the plays which suffered because of the frequent wanderings of the company. In a letter which Sarcey as usual published in the *Temps*, Antoine tried to explain the situation.

Interpretation with us ought to have only a secondary importance. I am far happier to have discovered *Les Fossiles* in a pile of manuscripts, and to have brought Curel to your attention than vexed at having played the piece badly. In that matter I am like the little, well-established shop-keepers who cannot afford to keep a clerk. I sweep the shop and I carry the letters myself. The essential thing is to continue assuring young writers of the certainty that their plays will be read and played, even very badly, for that is worth more to them than not to be played at all. These plays will ultimately find talented actors elsewhere.

Sarcey admitted the truth of Antoine's statements but insisted once more that, in spite of his good qualities, his influence had been baneful in many ways. The critic felt that even the diction of the actors of the sacrosanct Comédie-Française had been vitiated by the evil influence of the players of the Théâtre-Libre. In most of the plays of the Théâtre-Libre, argued Sarcey, the art of diction might well be suppressed, because the larger part of its plays were neither poetic nor artistic, and called for a matter-of-fact delivery on the part of the actor; but in tragedies like *Les Fossiles*, full of language of poetic beauty, the impression was painful. Then too Sarcey found fault with Antoine's realistic setting. He considered that, in a tragedy, the *mise-en-scène* should be as simple as possible, and the setting for *Les Fossiles* had been far from simple.

Curel's next play, *L'Invitée*, was put on with little success at the Vaudeville. Finally, in October, 1893, his *L'Amour brode* was accepted at the Comédie-Française, where it was hissed. It was played, according to Antoine, with a peculiar lack of understanding on the part of the actors. Antoine had been approached by a friend of Le Bargy, who played the part of the protagonist, Charles Méran, to use his influence in persuading Curel to make certain changes in the play. Whereupon Antoine poured upon Le Bargy's head the vials of his wrath in a stinging letter.

The misfortune is that you confuse without a doubt two arts that are absolutely distinct. I should like to try to convince you — and these reflections have no other purpose — that actors should have no theories about the works which they perform. Their business is merely to play them, to interpret, to the best of their ability, characters which they may fail to understand. They are in reality manikins, marionettes, more or less perfected in proportion to their talents, whom the author dresses and moves about at will. Certainly, after long years, they acquire at times a sort of material experience; they can tell an author why a character should come in or go out on the right rather than on the left, but in no case can they, or should they, without departing from their true function, try to modify a character or a dénouement.

The intellectual gap between the poet and his interpreter is so impassable that never can the latter satisfy the former. The actor always deforms the vision of the author who accepts a characterization that is nearly right, and who most often resigns himself to the impossible. . . . The absolute ideal of the actor should be to make himself a keyboard, an instrument, marvelously tuned, on which the author may play at will. It is sufficient for him to have a purely physical and technical training, to make his body, face, and voice more supple, and an intellectual training that will permit him to understand simply what the author would have him express. If it is asked of him to be sad or gay, he ought, to be a good comedian in the exact sense of the word, to express in masterly fashion, sadness or gaiety, without appreciating why these sentiments are demanded of him. That is the author's business, he knows what he is doing, and he is the only one who is responsible to the spectator. You will agree with me that the actor's art, thus reduced to its limits, still remains a conspicuously honorable and difficult one.

To return to your case, you were then wrong to criticize a play by a talented author of the free school of drama, because you know nothing about the sources of his inspiration. And as one cannot possibly do well two things at the same time, those extraneous preoccupations stood in your way, and made it impossible for you to give the author all that he has a right to expect from his interpreter, namely, sincerity and faith in the work which he has entrusted to your hands to be translated to the public.

Ten years after the writing of this letter it bore fruit. The committee of actors at the Comédie-Française which read and passed upon plays was abolished.

In December of 1892, a tour carried the Théâtre-Libre into Italy, where it was enthusiastically received, especially in Turin and in Milan. Antoine gave the Italians his most popular plays, *Blanchette*, *La Tante Léontine*, *Jacques Damour*, *La Dupe*, *L'École des veufs*, *La Fille Élisa*, *Ghosts*, *Les Fenêtres* by Perrin and Couturier, *Leurs Filles*, and *Deux Tourtereaux* of Ginisty and Guérin.

The Théâtre-Libre had introduced Tolstoy and Ibsen to French audiences. The next foreign dramatist to be represented on its stage was Strindberg with *Miss Julia*. Strindberg, half madman and half genius, who was for reforming everything under the sun, had very pronounced ideas on the drama. Inspired by Zola, who had written a preface to the first French edition of *The Father*, and by the Théâtre-Libre, he wrote a series of realistic plays which stand out as the sanest part of his literary work. His nomadic life had taken him to Paris several times, and he had written in 1891 a book on *The Associations of France and Sweden up to the Present Time*. Among his multifarious pursuits he had been an unsuccessful actor, and in 1889, with the assistance of his first wife and a group of students, he had started at Copenhagen an experimental theatre, still another offshoot of the Théâtre-Libre. The one and only play put on at Strindberg's theatre however was his own *Creditors*.

Miss Julia, which is to a certain extent an anti-Ibsen play, had been produced by the Freie Bühne in Berlin, and its preface had some influence on the Théâtre-Libre movement. Antoine considered this preface so important that he distributed translations of it on the night of the production of *Miss Julia*. In 1908, Strindberg gave an account of the genesis of his realistic plays.

In the 80's the new spirit of the times began to extend its demands for reform to the stage. Zola declared war against French comedy, with its Brussels carpets, its patent-leather shoes, its patent-leather themes, and its dialogue, which reminds one of the questions and answers of the catechism. In 1887, Antoine opened his Théâtre-Libre at Paris, and *Thérèse Raquin*, although nothing but an adapted novel, became the dominant model. It was the powerful theme and the concentrated form that showed innovation, although the unity of time was not yet observed, and curtain calls were retained. It was then that I wrote my dramas: *Miss Julia*, *The Father*, and *Creditors*.

The preface of *Miss Julia* shows the influence not only of the revolutionary movement in France, but also of that in Germany. To the Strindberg of 1888, just as was the case with Edmond de Goncourt in 1885, the drama of Europe was dying. In England and in Germany it was already dead and buried, and

in some other countries it has been thought possible to create a new drama by filling the old forms with the contents of a new time. But there has been no new form devised for the new contents, and the new wine has burst the old bottles.

Accordingly Strindberg in *Miss Julia* set about modernizing the form in accordance with the demands of the new time. We can omit the long explanation of his characters, because if an author has not expressed them adequately in his play, then he has failed in his purpose. Surely Dumas and Shaw have proved this point conclusively. In his dialogues Strindberg would avoid turning his characters into catechists who ask stupid questions in order to call forth witty answers. He claims to have avoided the symmetrical and mathematical construction of the French dialogue, and has permitted instead "minds to work irregularly as they do in reality." He confesses that he has taken as models "the monographic novels of the brothers de Goncourt, which have appealed to me more than any other modern literature."

Treating the technical side of the drama, he states that he has tried to abolish the division into acts

because I have come to fear that our decreasing capacity for illusion might be unfavorably affected by intermissions during which the spectator would have time to reflect and get away from the suggestive influence of the author-hypnotist.

If an audience can listen to a lecture or a sermon or a debate for a period of an hour and a half, it surely can listen to a play of that length. Strindberg had tried to abolish divisions into acts in a five-act play, *The Outlaw*, which he had burned because he judged its effect too scattered. As an experiment he provided resting places in the action of *Miss Julia* by introducing monologues, pantomime, and dances, "all of them belonging to the tragedy of classical antiquity." In spite of the dislike of the modern realists to the monologue, he defends it on the ground that "a servant-girl may talk to her cat, a mother may babble to her child, and an old spinster may prattle to her parrot." He advocates that monologues might at times be merely indicated and not written out in full, as is the case in certain Italian plays,

because the gifted actor, carried away by the situation and the mood of the occasion, may improvise such matters better than they could be written by the author, who cannot figure out in advance how much may be said, and how long the talk may last, without waking the public out of its illusions.

Pantomime is to be used when the monologue would seem unreal; and in order not to try the public beyond its endurance, he has introduced music, "which is amply warranted by the *Midsummer Night's Dream* dance."

As for scenery, Strindberg has borrowed the asymmetry and abruptness of the impressionists, in order to intensify his illusions. He would rid the stage of canvas doors and the painting of shelves and kitchen utensils on the walls. The walls might well be of canvas, but since he has only one setting, he wants it as real as possible, in view of the fact that at best there is so much on the stage that is conventional. In order that the actors may show full and half profile when sitting opposite each other at a table, he conceived the idea of making the rear wall diagonal.

Strindberg also advocated abolishing footlights. I have never been able to discover the inventor of those abominations nor have I been able to determine who was the first of the moderns to demand their removal. Was it Strindberg? Zola foresaw a time when they might be abolished, and it will be remembered that Antoine experimented with this innovation in *La Mort du duc d'Enghien* and in *La Patrie en danger*. Jean Jullien took up the cry in 1892, and the most progressive theatres of Paris have long abandoned this unnatural form of lighting. As for acting, Strindberg has no illusions about getting the actor to play *for* the public and not *at* it, although such a change would be highly desirable.

I dare not even dream [he says], of beholding the actor's back throughout an important scene, but I wish with all my heart that crucial scenes might not be played in the centre of the proscenium, like duets meant to bring forth applause.

He cannot hope that actresses be more lifelike than beautiful, but urges that actors at least use a minimum of make-up, because "in modern psychological dramas, the subtlest movements of the soul are reflected on the face rather than by gesture and noise."

Furthermore Strindberg would avoid the visible orchestra "with its disturbing lamps and its faces turned toward the public." He would have seats in the pit raised so that the eyes of the spectators would be above the knees of the actors.

If we could get rid of the boxes with their tittering parties of diners and if, first and last, we could have a small stage and a small house, then a new dramatic art might arise and the theatre might, at last, become an institution for the entertainment of people of culture. While waiting for this kind of theatre, I suppose we shall have to write for the "ice-box," and thus prepare the repertory that is to come. I have made an attempt. If it prove a failure, there is plenty of time to try over again.

Small wonder that Antoine went to the expense of translating this preface and distributing it to his audience. It had given him a great many suggestions for his outline for a new playhouse. It was another step forward toward the twentieth century "little" theatre that has become almost universal. Antoine had already introduced into France, either through plays or brochures, fresh ideas from Germany, Russia, Norway, and England; here was a new European voice added to the chorus, a voice from Sweden. Like Molière, Antoine might say, "Je prends mon bien où je le trouve."

In spite of the many ultra-realist plays that had preceded it at the Théâtre-Libre, *Miss Julia* created a considerable furor for the moment, but like all the other violent plays of its kind, it was soon forgotten. The French critics found nothing new in Strindberg except a few technical innovations. To them *Miss Julia* was merely another manifestation of brutal French realism. This was true. More than any other foreign dramatist, Strindberg follows Zola both in theory and practice. His characters quiver under the knife of the literary surgeon who dissects them cruelly, unmercifully. Yet *Miss Julia* is a finer work of art than many of the French ultra-realist plays of the Théâtre-Libre.

Edmond de Goncourt's *A bas le Progrès*, which was played the same evening as *Miss Julia*, pales into insignificance in comparison with the work of the foreigner who had evidently received so much inspiration from him and from his brother. Clearly the great days of the surviving Goncourt were numbered. *A bas le Progrès* is a puerile satire on contemporary France, and was one of the weakest plays in the whole repertory of the Théâtre-Libre. The printed version is preceded by a bombastic attack against foreign plays and a plea for a return to the manner of Beaumarchais. Goncourt's diatribes against Russian and Norwegian literatures are representative of the French chauvinist spirit which Antoine did so much to combat. It was not until after the war that this attitude on the part of the majority of the French critics was completely overcome.

Says Goncourt:

I have tried to react against the infatuation felt by France for foreign literature, against that idolatry of our young dramatic writers for the Scandinavian drama. They act as if they were the literary servants of Tolstoy and Ibsen, writers whose merit I am far from contesting, but whose qualities, in my opinion, cannot be acclimated to the degree of latitude in which we live. I have tried to write a play, as far as is within my power, with the French qualities of clearness, wit, and irony. Yes, I have a conviction that we ought to leave the Slavic mists to Russian and Norwegian minds and not try to introduce them by force into our own clear intellects.

I think that, transplanted in our land, the growth of this drama of
the north is sickly, and is likely to produce only clumsy plagiarisms.
And good Heavens! If our modern literature must absolutely have
an inspiration, French thought should turn neither to Ibsen nor
to Tolstoy, but rather to the author of the comedies, *Le Barbier de
Séville*, *Le Mariage de Figaro*, to the author of the drama *Eugénie*,
to Beaumarchais.

Poor Edmond! He had not yet caught up even with
Mme. de Staël on European literature, and as it happened, the Scandinavian play, produced at the same time
as his pseudo-Beaumarchaisian "bouffonnerie satirique,"
was as clear as a bell. European literary currents swing
back and forth. Strindberg owed as much to French
drama as he gave to it. Edmond de Goncourt had out-
lived himself as a dramatist and as a literary lawgiver.

The season of 1892 had given the Théâtre-Libre its
best tragedy in *Les Fossiles*. By a singular coincidence,
it also gave it its best comedy, *Boubouroche* of Georges
Courteline. Courteline had already written several comic
sketches and had produced his play in one act, *Lidoire*,
at the Théâtre-Libre in 1891. *Lidoire* is one of his many
skits on soldier life and is no more distinguished than
hundreds of contemporary farces. *Boubouroche* was his
second dramatic essay, this time a venture in two acts,
although he himself has stated that "one act, a single
act, that's my measure for the stage." *Boubouroche* is now
in the repertory of the Comédie-Française and is still as
popular as it was on the first night. For once critics and
public unanimously agreed that the Théâtre-Libre had
produced a masterpiece of farce.

Here is the "philosophy" of *Boubouroche* in the words
of Le Monsieur, who, in act one, informs Boubouroche
that his mistress is unfaithful to him.

All women can be summed up in that word "unfaithful." Take the word of an old philosopher who knows what he is talking about, and who has suffered the harsh experience of the apothegms that he utters. Men betray women in the modest proportion of one in every two; but women, women betray men in the terrible proportion of 97 per cent! Absolutely! 97! And that figure is no joke. It is proved by statistics and corroborated by the most elementary observation. In short, it may be for one reason or for another, or it may be for no reason at all, that at this very moment that I am talking to you, an intruder is under your roof; he is seated in your favorite arm-chair, he is warming his toes at the hearth which is accustomed to toast yours, and he is whistling over and over again the tune of the *Peace-maker* which he has learned from you who have sung it so often. Whether you believe a word of it or not, that is your right. As for me, my mission is fulfilled, and I withdraw with a light heart, feeling that I have done my duty without weakness, without hatred, and without fear. If men would introduce into their lives that spirit of solidarity which women have to such a high degree, and do for each other what I have just done for you, the number of cuckolds would not be lessened; but how simple, and that's the point that I'm driving at, how simple would be the delicate and complicated business of parting.

Act two is in the home of Adèle, Boubouroche's mis-tress. As the curtain goes up, sure enough, there is the "intruder" André, toasting his feet by the fireside. The bell rings several times. André scurries to a wardrobe which is conveniently lighted and provided with reading material. Finally "cet imbécile de Boubouroche" comes, discovers "the intruder," threatens at first to kill him, and then lets him go, rushing with murder in his eye at Adèle, only to fall upon her neck and accept her lame explanation that André's presence was made imperative by a family secret which she cannot reveal and about which he must not question her. All this notwithstanding the fact that André had presented his card and had gone through the polite motions of a man caught *in flagrante delicto*. The exquisite finishing touch is the beating which the tale-telling Monsieur receives for calumniating Adèle. *La Parisienne* was parody, *Boubouroche* is burlesque.

Hauptmann's *Weavers* was the next foreign play to invade the Théâtre-Libre. No foreign author owes more to Zola and to the Théâtre-Libre than Gerhart Hauptmann, the greatest dramatic poet of the European free-theatre movement. *The Weavers* made a special appeal to Antoine because it gave him another opportunity to show his skill with crowds on the stage. The starved, wretched weavers are the real protagonists of the play, and Antoine was once more successful in animating with life a large group of supernumeraries. *The Weavers* is a social treatise, dramatic propaganda if you will, but a work of art that is far superior to any similar dramatic work in France. It shows clearly the influence of Zola, Tolstoy, and the Théâtre-Libre. It was Hauptmann's third play produced at the Freie Bühne, and was at first prohibited by the censor because of its revolutionary tendencies. Antoine showed his usual *flair* in choosing *The Weavers*, which was the finest German play yet produced by the Théâtre-Libre of Berlin. In form it had much in common with *La Mort du duc d'Enghien* and *La Patrie en danger*, in that it is a series of detached scenes in which crowds play an important part.

Seldom does Antoine show himself so enthusiastic as when he speaks of the production of Hauptmann's play, the first German importation of the Théâtre-Libre.

The Weavers is an immense success. It must be conceded that no French dramatic author is capable of painting a fresco of such amplitude and power. The play, produced at the Théâtre-Libre of Berlin, had created an enormous stir. Hauptmann, behind whom all young literary Germany had placed itself, had succeeded in having the imperial interdict repealed. Here, contrary to what I had expected, that revolutionary play resounded like a cry of despair and wretchedness; from act to act, the audience, deeply moved, did not stop applauding. It is the masterpiece of a social drama which is still in its infancy.

Moreover, as I feel very strongly that this is one of the last spectacles in which I shall play and that the end of my effort is on the horizon, I put into it all the power, resources, and energy in me, and I can say that the interpretation was admirable. . . . All the second act, with the Song of the Weavers, which serves as a *leitmotiv* and rumbles continually behind the scene, had a prodigious effect. In the fourth act in the overrunning of the manufacturer's house, the illusion of terror was so intense that the whole orchestra stood up. The last tableau, with the death of old Hilse in the fusillade, and the noise of the crowd, was carried out amid applause.

In spite of its artistic success, *The Weavers* marked the beginning of the end of Antoine's venture. The Théâtre-Libre had reached its high-water mark. Were it not that a friend had advanced Antoine a thousand francs, the production of the play would have been impossible. This was the last performance but one of the season, and if he had not already engaged himself to produce other plays, Antoine would have ended his enterprise with this season of 1892–1893.

My own energy and courage are not enough to carry on [he writes]. Up to the present moment I have drawn from myself and from my friends, authors and actors, all that we have in us, but money I cannot fabricate. I have threatened too many interests, disturbed too many people in high places to expect anything but general satisfaction when I shall be found to be at the end of my rope. . . . To tell the truth I feel that from the artistic point of view, we are coming to the end of our tether and that our movement is doomed. For two years I have had to appeal to foreign drama, to sensational curiosities, to fill up the intervals of our own really fine work, but all that is exhausted. . . . The Théâtre-Libre, if it is to maintain itself on the plane on which it started, cannot mean anything unless it is fed by a national production. Now the authors who began with us have gone elsewhere.

The season of 1892–1893 ended with a cry of despair from Antoine, yet it had produced the two greatest French plays of the Théâtre-Libre, *Les Fossiles* and *Boubouroche*, and had made known to France a great German play which was unquestionably inspired by the Théâtre-Libre. Curel and Hauptmann are the two greatest glories of the Théâtre-Libre movement, which had become by this time a European institution and was no longer exclusively French.

CHAPTER XI

THE LAST OF THE THEATRE–LIBRE AND AFTER
(1893–1896)

AFTER such strong doses of foreign realism as the *Power of Darkness*, *Ghosts*, and *Miss Julia*, and such a beautiful bit of dramatic poetry as *The Weavers*, Björnson's *Bankruptcy* struck Antoine's audiences as being very tame. And it was. There is nothing original about *A Bankruptcy*, which had been on the repertory of the wandering Meininger. It is by no means Björnson's best, although it is his most popular play. In construction it resembles closely the work of Augier and Dumas, and indeed it belongs to their epoch, having been written in 1874. In spirit it is more akin to Augier than to Dumas in that it extols the homely virtues of the Norwegian people. "All's well that ends well," in *A Bankruptcy*. A dishonest financier sees the error of his ways, reforms, and brings happiness to his family. Antoine probably hit upon *A Bankruptcy* as a concession to the critics who had accorded Björnson a much overrated position and who regarded him during the eighties as a rival to Ibsen.

Hauptmann shared with Ibsen the honor of being played twice at the Théâtre-Libre, and justly, since they were the two greatest European dramatists of the epoch. In November, Antoine went to Berlin to see the German production of the *Assumption of Hannele Mattern* which he himself was planning to give. He was received very cordially in Germany, especially by Hauptmann and

Sudermann who had formed a committee to receive him. During his week's stay he saw a great deal of the German theatres and was constantly struck by the mechanical superiority of German playhouses. He witnessed a performance of *The Weavers* which he found inferior to that of the Théâtre-Libre in point of view of acting. He was impressed by the fact that the German drama was not so centralized as in France, and that Dresden, Munich, and Leipzig, were almost as important dramatically as Berlin. He was given a banquet by the dramatic and artistic world of Berlin, where the Théâtre-Libre was held in very high honor. As to the performance of *Hannele*, he thought the piece extremely well played but felt sure that he could do better himself in the matter of stage-setting.

In February *Hannele* was performed in Paris. It did not make so much of a sensation as *The Weavers*, but Antoine felt that he had achieved a distinct success technically, as this dream-play demanded great skill on the part of the producer. With *Hannele*, Hauptmann made a definite break from the "naturalist" school. In it was foreshadowed the poet that he proved himself to be in *The Sunken Bell*, a work which made him recognized as the greatest living dramatist. *Hannele* is a combination of the realistic and the symbolic. It proved that a great poet could make great drama out of realistic elements. It was the last important play of the Théâtre-Libre, and illustrates better than any other work of that theatre the trend of the times. Hauptmann began as a disciple of the Zola-Becque school, and evolved a drama belonging to no school, a drama that followed the highest form of the German traditions set by Lessing, Schiller, and Goethe.

Une Journée parlementaire of the much overrated Maurice Barrès, which had been forbidden the professional stage, is yet another of the literary curiosities of the Théâtre-Libre. Although Antoine was not in sympathy with Barrès's political creed, he produced this political pamphlet which naturally furnished a great deal of newspaper copy. It is the only play that Barrès ever wrote, and though faulty in construction, nevertheless contains forceful elements. *Une Journée parlementaire* was probably based on an actual political scandal and aimed to show the venality and corruption in modern politics. Lemaître had set the fashion for political satire in his *Député Leveau* and Brieux had just finished his *Engrenage* which he wanted Antoine to take. But Antoine evidently thought that Brieux was able to make his way on the legitimate stage, or that the *Journée parlementaire* would give him more prestige, so he chose the latter. The production was disastrously expensive, and because of lack of funds, Antoine was unable to give a performance in March.

This was the first time since the inauguration of regular seasons in October, 1887, that the Théâtre-Libre had failed to give its monthly programme. Antoine was now flying with one wing, and in April gave his last performance. Besides having the distinction of being the last play produced by Antoine at the Théâtre-Libre, *Le Missionnaire* also belongs to the long line of curios of Antoine's venture. It is called by its author, one Marcel Luguet, a "roman théâtral en cinq tableaux." In this dramatic novel Antoine acted as chorus and interrupted the action to explain the state of soul of the characters. We have since become accustomed to this species of drama, and sit in bored apathy while the reader reads, but the audience of the Théâtre-Libre took the innovation as a huge joke, and howled Antoine down whenever he attempted to carry out his part of the programme. One individual even threw a handful of coins in his face.

Harassed and fatigued, Antoine, then and there, resolved to give up the battle. A few days later he announced his intention of closing the Théâtre-Libre temporarily. In June he turned over the theatre to Larochelle, son of the director of the Théâtre Cluny, with the understanding that two plays that had already been contracted for should be given.

A tour under the conduct of a manager took him and his troupe to Belgium, Germany, and Italy, where the company found itself stranded.

Here finishes the Odyssey of the Théâtre-Libre [says Antoine]. Starting seven years ago in my attic room in the Rue Dunquerque, with forty cents in my pocket, to go and rehearse our first performance at the little wine-shop in the Rue des Abbesses, I find myself in Rome possessing about the same sum, surrounded by some fifteen comrades just as discomfited as myself, with a hundred thousand franc debt awaiting me in Paris, and not knowing what we shall do on the morrow.

Larochelle's directorship was a poor substitute for Antoine's pioneer work. For some reason or other no plays were performed until February of the following year, a hiatus of ten months. Three performances still due to Antoine's subscribers were given in 1895, and five during the season of 1895–1896. Although the great names of Villiers de L'Isle-Adam and Maupassant are found on Larochelle's programmes, the two outstanding plays given by him were Fabre's *L'Argent*, and *Le Cuivre* of Paul Adam and André Picard. Fabre's play had been accepted by Antoine as far back as 1892, but had not been produced. *L'Argent* is dedicated to Becque, who is Fabre's master, and reminds one in the first act of *Les Corbeaux*. In *Les Corbeaux*, however, there are a few rays of sunshine. *L'Argent* is all blackness and hopelessness. A father who manufactures adulterated chocolate, is deceived by his wife who has been the mistress of his banker. His son of twenty-five is a ne'er-do-well, and has had a child by the housemaid. The daughter is a heartless wretch ready to squeeze every sou from her mother, and the son-in-law is an avaricious and unscrupulous blackguard. The weakest part of this melodrama is the discovery of the stage letter which reveals· the secret between the merchant's wife and his banker. The whole thing is exaggerated, yet in it the power of money over men's souls is well analyzed. Lemaître called it the best naturalist play of the Théâtre-Libre and credited it with being more sincere than most of its congeners. In *L'Argent* Antoine made his final appearance as an actor at the Théâtre-Libre.

Le Cuivre is one of the most honorable failures of the Théâtre-Libre. It is an unsuccessful attempt at a play of ideas with the sex element running through it as an obligato. The main thought behind *Le Cuivre* is that wars are engineered by private business concerns, an idea which gives it quite a post-war flavor, and that the most honorable of men may fall into the snares of unscrupulous women and make blackguards of themselves. There are three love affairs which complicate the machinery of *Le Cuivre*. One an adulterous love which is the outcome of the obsessing tactics of a Don Juan and the cynical suspicion of a husband. The second is the romantic love of a maid for an officer whom she will not accept until he gives up his military career. When he does so he is immediately shot. The third and most curious is the animal love of a cerebral female for an idealist who is undone by the wiles of the siren, and who goes mad when he visualizes the consequences of his actions. There is material for three or more plays in *Le Cuivre*, which is extremely well written and which deserved a better fate than was meted out to it.

It was in October, 1894, that Antoine found himself stranded in Rome. In January of 1895 he appeared at the Gymnase, playing in Lemaître's *Age Difficile*. In May of the same year he helped Larochelle put on Fabre's *Argent* and took a part in the performance. In March, 1896, he was at the Renaissance with Lucien Guitry, playing in Curel's *Figurante*. A little later during that same year he was made co-director of the Odéon with Ginisty, but resigned soon after his appointment because of disagreements with his colleague, who had suggested him as director four years previously. After a long foreign tour which took him to South America, he returned to France, and with the help of some of his loyal Théâtre-Libre friends went back to the Menus-Plaisirs with the idea of continuing the Théâtre-Libre as a public playhouse. Larochelle, however, was unwilling to yield the name which he declared was now his property. But that was a minor matter. In the eyes of the public, Antoine was the Théâtre-Libre and the Théâtre-Libre was Antoine, and on the evening of September 30, 1897, he opened the Menus-Plaisirs under the name of the Théâtre Antoine. The first performance included *Boubouroche* and *Blanchette*, which combination of Théâtre-Libre plays now appears together on the repertory of the Comédie-Française.

At the Théâtre Antoine the work of the Théâtre-Libre was to a certain extent carried on for the general public for a period of nine years. It is interesting to see what plays of the old Théâtre-Libre survived. In the first place Antoine revived *La Parisienne*, as he had promised to do. Becque was also represented by *Les Honnêtes Femmes*. Antoine also resurrected that one-act jewel, *La Révolte*. Ibsen, Tolstoy, Hauptmann, Strindberg, and Björnson reappeared. Of the so-called naturalist plays, he repeated *Sœur Philomène*, *La Fille Élisa*, *La Dupe*, *L'Ecole des veufs*, *Jacques Damour*, *La Tante Léontine*, *Rolande*, *L'Argent*, and *Leurs filles*. *La Mort du duc d'Enghien* and *Les Fenêtres* appeared on his programme once more, and of the plays in verse he revived *La Nuit Bergamasque*, *L'Amante du Christ*, Marsolleau's *Son petit cœur*, and Vaucaire's *Un beau soir*, *Le Baiser* having been taken by the Comédie-Française. Besides *Blanchette*, Brieux furnished four plays.   Curel also gave four. *Les Fossiles* had gone to the Comédie-Française.

In 1906 Antoine was made director of the Odéon without an associate. Here he remained until shortly before the outbreak of the World War in 1914. Antoine revolutionized that government playhouse physically as well as dramatically, but his hands were tied, more or less, in his capacity as a state functionary. He welcomed young playwrights, however, and alternated their plays with those of the world's greatest dramatists, Æschylus, Sophocles, Shakespeare, Calderón, Goethe, and Schiller, as well as those of the great French classic writers. He had the delicacy not to obtrude his Théâtre-Libre plays by French authors, but repeated the works of Tolstoy, Hauptmann, and Ibsen. The precursors of the Théâtre-

Libre, Balzac, Flaubert, Daudet, Villiers de L'Isle-Adam, Zola, and Becque, all found their way into his repertory. In 1914 he resigned, with a colossal debt, and, as Rostand whimsically put it, went to Constantinople "chez les Teurs." Since the war Antoine has taken a fly in the movies with Daudet's *Arlésienne*, an episode which is facetiously described by René Benjamin in his *Antoine Déchaîné*. For several years he has been a dramatic critic, a field into which he accidentally stumbled. To-day he is the acknowledged pope of French drama, the unofficial adviser of playwrights, directors, and actors.

CHAPTER XII

THE INFLUENCE OF THE THEATRE-LIBRE

I. THE THÉÂTRE-LIBRE AND FRENCH DRAMA

ZOLA had made the air ring with protestations and formulas for a new drama. Musset had already shown that French plays could be cast into new moulds. Balzac, the Goncourts, Villiers de l'Isle-Adam, and Daudet were the forerunners of the revolutionary tendencies. Becque finally forced an unwilling recognition of the free drama, and Antoine fought and won the fight for it. The Théâtre-Libre was essentially a fighting theatre, it was not a commercial enterprise. And when the playwrights of the new movement found a paying market elsewhere, when amateur actors of the Théâtre-Libre found positions in the regular theatres, when innovations in acting and stage-setting had been accepted even at the Comédie-Française, then "the day of pistol shots" had passed. Antoine was ready for a regular playhouse, where concessions would be made to the general public.

It is a fallacy to suppose that the so-called neo-romantic drama and the plays of the symbolists put an end to the free-theatre movement. Mendès, Aicard, and Banville, all of them poets, gave plays to the Théâtre-Libre. Rostand, Richepin, Claudel, and Bouchor produced successful plays in verse elsewhere during the life of the Théâtre-Libre. France has always had and always will have her drama in verse. Corneille, Racine, and Molière, Victor Hugo and Rostand, always attract large audi-

ences. The year 1898, when Rostand's *Cyrano de Bergerac*
appeared for the first time, has been set by many critics
as the date of the fall of the free theatre movement in
France. This theory is based on false suppositions.
Maeterlinck, the symbolist, had been saluted already in
1889 as the Belgian Shakespeare, and Rostand came into
conspicuous notice as early as 1894 with his *Romanesques*.
Neither the symbolist movement nor the neo-romantic
movement has borne fruit, but the end of the free dramatic movement is not yet. The French Théâtre-Libre
was the cradle of the "little" theatres which have swept
all over the western world. They have just begun to
penetrate the dramatic wilderness of the United States.

The Théâtre-Libre may not have been the first amateur group of dramatic reformers in latter-day Paris, but
Antoine put upon it his distinguishing mark and made it
famous throughout the world. The Cercle des Escholiers
was contemporaneous with it. The Théâtre Indépendent,
the Théâtre de l'Application, the Théâtre d'Art all existed
during its lifetime, but these are mere names now, and
can be found only in detailed treatises on French drama.

The most famous successor of the Théâtre-Libre was
Lugné-Poe's Théâtre de l'Oeuvre, which was founded in
1893. This theatre suspended its activities during the
course of the war, but still continues to play to small
private audiences. Lugné-Poe served his apprenticeship
under Antoine during the years 1888–1890, when he acted
in about a dozen plays of the Théâtre-Libre under the
pseudonym of Philipon. When Paul Fort, self-styled
"prince of poets," founded the Théâtre d'Art in 1891,
Lugné-Poe joined that enterprise, and in 1893 founded
the Oeuvre, which opened with a performance of Maeter-

linck's *Pelléas et Mélisande*, and became more or less a
rival of the Théâtre-Libre. The Oeuvre may be said to be
carrying on to this day the work of Antoine in making
Paris more hospitable to foreign plays. Ibsen, who has
become a sort of fetish with Lugné-Poe, Hauptmann,
Strindberg, Björnson, Oscar Wilde, Gogol, Schnitzler,
and d'Annunzio have all been played at the Oeuvre.
Lugné-Poe has travelled extensively and has carried
French plays to remote parts of the world. The striking
difference between Antoine and Lugné-Poe is that the
former was a total failure as a theatrical business man
whereas the latter has been eminently successful. Lugné-
Poe affirms that conducting a playhouse is a business
like any other.

But the Paris theatre that more nearly fills the place
of the Théâtre-Libre is Copeau's Vieux Colombier,
opened in 1914. A small public theatre, it has given to
Paris audiences most finished performances of French and
foreign plays, classic as well as modern. Much of its repertory was made familiar to American audiences in its two
seasons of exile in New York during the World War.
Antoine and Lugné-Poe have had too many private disagreements to render justice to each other. Of the Vieux
Colombier, Antoine has said that it has "too much of
a literary flavor attached to it," yet when he saw there
Vildrac's *Le Paquebot Tenacity* in 1922, he exclaimed,
"The future belongs to the Vieux Colombier." If it is
true that Copeau has been forced to suspend his activities
because of financial difficulties, as recent reports seem to
indicate, then French drama will have suffered a tremendous loss, for the Vieux Colombier is not only a
theatre, it is a dramatic university. It has a dramatic

school, it gives public lectures on literature and music, it has a workshop of its own. Then, too, it has carried French plays beyond the confines of France. So high are the ideals of Copeau that he does not hope to have a perfect troupe until he shall have trained from childhood a group of students now studying at his dramatic school.

The Vieux Colombier too has had its offshoots. Dullin, who began with Antoine at the Odéon, but who perfected himself with Copeau, is struggling with his interesting experiment, the Atelier of Montmartre. Jouvet, formerly with the Vieux Colombier, was until recently associated with Pitoëff at the Comédie des Champs-Élysées, where some of the most artistic plays of contemporary drama have been performed. The Comédie des Champs-Élysées enjoys the distinction of being the most beautiful theatre of Paris, possessing a proscenium and auditorium that are as simple and as austere as those of the Greeks. It is interesting to note in passing that not one of these three playhouses uses footlights. They are more receptive to foreign authors and to new ideas than any other theatre of Paris with the exception of the Oeuvre.

Firmin Gémier began his career with Antoine in 1887 in an insignificant rôle of *La Femme de Tabarin*, but left the Théâtre-Libre troupe to play elsewhere. His real success as an actor dates from his portrayal of Bonenfant in Brieux's *Blanchette*, performed in February, 1892. From then until the closing days of the Théâtre-Libre he was one of its leading spirits. Later he became Antoine's right-hand man at the Théâtre Antoine, where he succeeded his chief as director in 1906. He is now director of the Odéon, having once more followed in Antoine's wake. In spite of Gémier's close attachment to Antoine, he has developed further away from him in his dramatic ideals than any of Antoine's former associates. Like Romain Rolland, Gémier has become fired with the project of a theatre for the people, and now directs the popular-priced plays and operas given under government auspices in the huge hall of the Trocadéro. He is intensely interested in pageants and has done some very beautiful work in open-air theatres. He is a mountain of energy, but has a tendency to dissipate it with his multifarious interests.

At the Comédie-Française reigns a by-product of Antione, Émile Fabre, author of *L'Argent* of Théâtre-Libre days, and one of the founders of the Théâtre-Libre of Marseilles. Thus two men intimately connected with the Théâtre-Libre, the destroyer of conventions, are guiding the destinies of France's two state theatres.

Still another product of the Théâtre-Libre is Rodolphe Darzens, for a long period archivist of that theatre, author of one of its plays, translator of Ibsei.'s *Ghosts*, and compiler of an anecdotic history of its season of 1889–1890. He too is now a director. At the Théâtre des Arts he is performing the hitherto impossible feat of making François de Curel popular.

While speaking of Antoine's lieutenants who have made themselves famous, it would not be just to pass over in silence the work of the modest Mlle. Barny. She was one of the most indefatigable and talented of all his assistants. She helped him organize the original troupe, stayed with him through thick and thin until his resignation in 1893, followed him to the Odéon and to the Théâtre Antoine. She frequently played the part of the *mère* to Antoine's *père*, creating sixty-six rôles during her seven years' service at the Théâtre-Libre. She became a model to actresses in Paris for so-called character parts. In moments of despair it was Mlle. Barny who bolstered up Antoine's faltering courage.

In the face of these facts, it is nonsense to say that the Théâtre-Libre was swept away by the neo-romantics and symbolists. They have passed and gone and left no trace, whereas a modified, restrained Théâtre-Libre ideal rules French drama to-day.

2. THE THÉÂTRE-LIBRE AND GERMAN DRAMA

Of all the dramas of modern Europe, that of Germany owes more to France than to any other nation. Inspired by Zola's theories and by the twin German Zolas, Holz and Schlaf, as well as by the brave struggle of Antoine, young Germany produced a Freie Bühne, a Free Stage, and Hauptmann. The German dramatists of the eighteen-seventies and eighties, like those of many another country of Europe, either translated, adapted, or took as models, the works of the famous French triumvirate, Dumas, Augier, and Sardou. Even Ohnet had his worshippers, and the lesser lights of the Paris boulevard theatres were almost as popular in Germany as in France. So complete was the French dramatic invasion of Berlin that one critic seriously proposed the enactment of a protective tariff against it. Germany had conquered France in war, but the German theatre had abjectly surrendered to that of France.

Every evening [said one German critic] the French mind wins brilliant victories over German thought and sentiment, and our poets are happy when they can pick up the crumbs from the table of their rich neighbor.

The plays of Lindau, Kotzebue, and Blumenthal, the most popular of the German purveyors of the French manner of this period, are perhaps more moral than those of their models, but they are infinitely duller. Dumas paid Lindau the doubtful compliment of saying that he was just as French in spirit as if he were born in France. Of the more original writers, Paul Heyse was not primarily a dramatist, and Wilbrandt, director as well as playwright, adapted Greek tragedies and presented stereotyped historical plays. Wildenbruch, the most thoroughly German of the dramatists of the eighteen-seventies and eighties, tried with his verse tragedies to evoke the spirit of the past in pale imitations of Schiller. The greatest contributions made by Germany to European drama during the two barren decades that followed the Franco-Prussian War were the acting of the Meininger, who revolutionized the stage in Germany, and the late drama-operas of Wagner.

Neither the historical plays of Wildenbruch nor the technique of the Meininger satisfied the young bloods of Berlin, who were looking for something new and fresh as heralded by the theories of Zola, and the plays of Ibsen, Tolstoy, and Strindberg. These foreign influences were the most potent in shaping the revolt that began to be strongly felt in the late eighties, a revolt that was called by later critics the new *Sturm und Drangperiode* of Germany, because it was not only the drama that was languishing, but the other literary arts as well. As early as 1882, the brothers Hart, Heinrich and Julius, had founded the review, *Kritische Waffengänge*, in which they asserted that German letters were but a faint echo of their country's classic literature and a base imitation of

French models. Among the young Berlin writers who allied themselves with this movement were Arno Holz and Hauptmann.

In 1885, Michael Conrad, who was deeply imbued with Zola's ideas, started another review, the *Gesellschaft*, in which the exponents of the conventional school were satirized and in which the call was sounded for new art and new literature. In the same year Karl Bleibtreu, who in his plays was paving the way for a revolt, launched a pamphlet entitled, *Literary Revolution*. Clubs and societies began to be formed in which these new hopes and theories were discussed. Of these the *Durch* was the most prominent. There Adalbert von Hanstein, author of *Das Yüngste Deutschland*, the most authoritative work on this period, read a paper on the drama of the future. In poetry and in the novel, Holz, Conrad, Alberti, Sudermann, and Hauptmann began to make their voices heard. And, although the new Deutschestheater was founded in 1882 by the dramatist L'Arronge, and the Lessingtheater came into being in 1888 headed by Blumenthal, still the youthful dramatists received no encouragement from either. The directors of these new theatres, which contributed in a general way to the renascence of German drama, were mainly interested in their own plays and in those of their conservative group.

But the spirit of dramatic revolution was in the air. Arno Holz, who had been working for some time on theories, began to bring about actual results. He was familiar with the works of Taine and Zola, and had visited the latter during his sojourn in France. Holz is the father of the modern dramatic movement in Germany, and if he did not himself produce lasting works, he inspired Hauptmann, who did. Holz reminds one of the Goncourts: "il s'emballe," as the French have it, he loses his sense of balance at times and writes utter nonsense. But he dealt sledge-hammer blows at the conventional style of his fellow German dramatists, and urged them to use the more vivid language of everyday life. Although he imbibed a great deal from Zola, he did not always agree with him. Whilst this young poet was tearing his hair over the nature and laws of art, trying like a new Descartes to sweep the literary past aside, start from a new basis, and create a more "consistent naturalism" than that of Zola, there came to visit him his friend Johannes Schlaf, a young philological student. After four years of collaboration they presented their new philosophy in the review *Neue Gleise*, New Tracks. In 1889 they did more than theorize, they created the first "naturalist" literary work in Germany, *Papa Hamlet*. The title is derived from the first of three tales written in the French manner of the *roman dialogué,* a species of narrative closely bordering on drama. These stories they published under the pseudonym of Bjarne P. Holmsen, and passed them off as translations of a Norwegian named Frantzius, a hoax which remained undiscovered for several months. In *Papa Hamlet*, as von Hanstein says, the young authors have out-Zolaed Zola, "Zola überzolat," with their meticulous descriptions and realistic language. Zola, as we know, never carried out his own dramatic theories. Holz and Schlaf are as extreme as any of the writers of the *comédie rosse* of the Théâtre-Libre.

The labors of these youthful enthusiasts might have had no influence on the drama in Germany but for the fact that Hauptmann chanced to see the manuscript of these stories as well as that of a play which they were working on, entitled *Die Familie Selicke*. Hauptmann had previously published a few poems and a novelette of Zolaist tendencies, but his acquaintance with Holz and Schlaf turned him toward the drama and became a decisive influence in his life. Holz offered to collaborate with him in a play that had begun to germinate in Hauptmann's mind, but the latter preferred to pay his debt by prefacing to his first play, *Before Sunrise*, the lines, "dedicated in joyful gratitude to Bjarne P. Holmsen, consistent realist, author of *Papa Hamlet*, through whose book I received a decisive stimulation."

The year 1889 was a red-letter epoch in the annals of German dramatic literature. Not only did it see the publication of *Papa Hamlet:* it was the year of the establishment of the Freie Bühne, the German Théâtre-Libre, and of the publication and presentation of Hauptmann's *Before Sunrise*, the first German play of the Freie Bühne. In January of that same year, Bernhard Westenberger had expressed the hope that Germany might soon have a Dichterbühne, a theatre for poets. As if in answer to that wish, Theodor Wolff and Maximilien Harden, then rising young journalists, who had been following with great interest the experiments of Antoine, invited a group of friends to discuss the organization of a similar institution for Germany. A committee of nine was formed with the young critic, Otto Brahm, as president. Because of differences of opinion, Harden and Wolff, who had originally instigated the idea, withdrew from active participation. From the very first it was apparent that Brahm dominated the group and brooked no opposition. S. Fischer, the publisher, was made treasurer, and the Brothers Hart,

Paul Schlenther, and Fritz Mauthner, all critics, Julius Stettenheim, the humorist, Paul Jonas, the lawyer, and Emmanuel Reicher, the actor, made up the famous nine. Taking as their model the French Théâtre-Libre, the youthful lovers of the drama drew up the following manifesto:

> It is the plan of those assembled to found a stage, independent of any of the existing theatres, yet not in rivalry with them, which shall be free from the censorship and from financial preoccupations. There shall be given during the theatrical season, in one of the leading playhouses of Berlin, about ten performances of modern plays of outstanding interest which, because of their nature, might find difficulty in being presented elsewhere. In the selection of these dramatic works, as well as in their presentation, our aim shall be to strive for a living art which shall be free from all virtuosity.

So quotes Paul Schlenther, one of the founders, in his brochure, "*Wozu der Lärm, Genesis der Freien Bühne* (What's all the to-do about? The Origin of the Free Stage).

Brahm and the "nine" began their work during the summer, and on the afternoon of September 29, 1889, presented Ibsen's *Ghosts* at the Lessingtheater. *Ghosts* had been previously presented in Berlin but had been withdrawn by the censor. In spite of the arguments of the more patriotic and hopeful enthusiasts against starting the revolt with a foreign play, the "nine" planned a programme of more foreign works by the Goncourts, Tolstoy, Björnson, and Strindberg. Meanwhile Brahm, who had insisted that no German play worthy of presentation had been received, suddenly came into possession of a manuscript by an unknown author, strongly recommended by the veteran Theodor Fontane. The presentation of Hauptmann's *Before Sunrise* was awaited with feverish excitement. It had been published by Fischer, and had set the dramatic world of Berlin on fire. The date of its first performance, October 20, 1889, was considered by the younger critics as important to German drama as that of *Hernani* had been to the French. It was certainly as uproarious an event. Reicher, the leading actor of the young troupe, exclaimed on reading the play:

How long have I desired to introduce this style of interpretation! How often have I purposely cut over-styled speeches in order to make my characters more natural! Here at last I come upon something I have long aspired to do.

Before Sunrise owes much to Holz and Schlaf as to technique, but it also shows unmistakable signs of the influence of Zola, Ibsen, and Tolstoy. Like *L'Assommoir* and *The Power of Darkness*, it presents a sordid picture of the terrible effects of alcoholism; like Ibsen's *Ghosts* it is based on the influence of heredity. It is even more of a tract than *The Power of Darkness* because one of its chief characters, Loth, who is really the mouthpiece of the author, is a reformer. Hauptmann shows in this youthful work a decided bent toward the thesis play. Alfred Loth, idealist as well as reformer, jilts his sweetheart, Helen, when he finds that she is the daughter of an inveterate drunkard and sister of a married woman who is herself a dipsomaniac, and who has already transmitted her disease to a child. Having sworn to preserve his future children from the effects of this horrible hereditary disease, Loth throws over Helen, who commits harikari in the most approved realistic style. Yet in spite of its theses and antitheses, *Before Sunrise* was a brave beginning. It gave German drama something that it had not possessed before, a realistic portrayal of modern bourgeois family life.

The third play of the Freie Bühne was the old war-horse of the free school of drama, *Henriette Maréchal*, which had been translated by Mauthner. As one German critic put it, this play of the Goncourts must have been chosen because of its truculent preface rather than for its dramatic merits. It was received rather coldly by an audience which had already tasted twice of ultra-realism. Tolstoy's *Power of Darkness* gave discriminating critics an opportunity to see how much Hauptmann had been indebted to the Russian. Anzengruber's *Fourth Estate*, which had never been seen in Germany, was a study of peasant life done in the old manner, and passed unnoticed.

Then came *Die Familie Selicke* of Holz and Schlaf, which had already played its influential part in the German revolutionary movement. From the naturalistic dramatic stories of these collaborators to this slice of family life was a short step. Neither of the two authors, however, was essentially a dramatist. Their formless staccato style, which in accordance with their theories should give a sensation of real life, their fierce preoccupation in avoiding that "papierne Sprache," literary style, makes the play tedious. Their chief title to glory rests on the inspiration they gave to the free-theatre movement in Germany, especially to Hauptmann, who was a dramatist before he was a theorist, and who avoided their excesses.

Arthur Fitger's *By the Grace of God* was another resurrected play, written in 1883, which had been forbidden by the censor because of its subversive political ideas. Brahm realized that his public, now educated to the outspoken language of the ultra-realist plays, cared naught for conventional style and technique, no matter how revolutionary the play might be in substance. The last performance of the season was Hauptmann's second play, *The Reconciliation*, in which incompatibility between husband and wife brings family dissensions. More complicated in plot than *Before Sunrise*, and still more concerned with theories of heredity, it failed to win the enthusiasm of the audience.

Thus ended the first season of the Freie Bühne. It had done what it set out to do. It had paved the way for a free German drama, and what was more important, it had discovered a new dramatist. During the first year the subscribers of the new theatre rose to the number of 700, and it had provoked so much interest that it was found necessary to have a magazine for the discussion of the plays and their authors. In January, 1890, from the house of Fischer, there appeared the first number of *Freie Bühne für Modernes Leben*, edited by Brahm and Holz, which became the organ of the dramatic movement.

One of the external influences which contributed no little to the success of the Freie Bühne was the appearance in 1889 of Sudermann's *Honor*, which was played shortly after the presentation of *Before Sunrise*. It had been published in 1888, and so was in no way connected with the theatre of the "nine." Sudermann, in fact, never identified himself with the Freie Bühne, and although his *Honor*, *Sodom's End*, and *Heimat*, universally known as *Magda*, were realistic enough in plot and character, they clung to the outworn technique of the Dumas school of drama. Their popular success, however, gave a tremendous impetus to the free-drama movement, and in spite of his detractors Sudermann deserves no little glory for his share in the development of an indigenous drama of modern German life.

During its first season the Freie Bühne had presented only one French play. Of the seven plays of the second season, two were French, both cornerstones of the free drama in France, Zola's *Thérèse Raquin* and Becque's *Corbeaux*. Strindberg's *Father* was the only other foreign play. The outstanding German play was Hauptmann's *Lonely Lives*, a psychological study of a dilettante and idealist who is unable to reconcile himself to things as they are and commits suicide.

After two years of fighting for a recognition of free drama, the organizers of the Freie Bühne considered that the battle had been won, and decided to produce only plays of exceptional value which might be refused elsewhere. *Lonely Lives* had been accepted at the Deutsches-theater; the enemy had capitulated. In 1892, the Freie Bühne produced Strindberg's *Miss Julia*, and in 1893, Hauptmann's *Weavers*, the finest work that the young German dramatist had yet written. In 1894, the Freie Bühne ceased to exist; Otto Brahm had been made direc-or of the Deutschestheater, thus receiving official recognition long before Antoine went to the Odéon. A new company was formed with Reicher as chief actor, and the doors of the theatre which was soon to become one of the leading playhouses of Europe were thrown open to all German dramatists of merit.

Just as the Théâtre-Libre had inspired free theatres in provincial France, so was the case with the Freie Bühne in Germany. Shortly after the foundation of the Freie Bühne, Conrad, Bleibtreu, and Alberti, not having been asked to join, organized in pique a rival theatre, the

Deutsche Bühne, where plays by Bleibtreu and Alberti were performed. But it was unable to compete with the Freie Bühne and was soon dissolved. In 1890 a second offshoot, the Freie Volksbühne, came into existence. Its purpose as stated by its founder, Bruno Wille, was social and instructive rather than literary and artistic, but it survived its model. It produced plays for the working classes at the very moderate cost of ten cents. These plays were neither exclusively realistic, nor classic, nor romantic. Wille believed that the masses could be re-generated only by appealing to the spiritual side of life, and chose his plays with this idea in view. The Freie Volksbühne, in its turn, split into two factions in 1895. That phenomenon illustrates the history of the whole movement in Germany. One free theatre begot another. In Munich, in Leipzig, in Breslau, in Hamburg, and in Vi-enna, theatres sprang up in emulation of the original Freie Bühne in Berlin. In Vienna, Schlenther, one of the most original spirits of the "nine," became director of the Burgtheater.

An extremely illuminating study might be made of the interplay of influences between the French and German drama during the last half of the nineteenth century. Antoine had been inspired by the acting and stage-setting of the Meininger, and by the Wagner theatre at Bay-reuth, as well as by the mechanics of the German theatres which he had studied in Berlin when he went to see Hauptmann's *Hannele Mattern* in 1894. On the other hand, Dumas and Zola were almost as well known in Germany as in France, and Zola was the chief inspiration of Holz. The Théâtre-Libre begot the Freie Bühne, and out of the Freie Bühne came modern Germany's greatest dramatist,

Hauptmann. Hauptmann in turn was the only foreign author except Ibsen whom Antoine played twice. As a matter of fact, the *Weavers* and *Hannele Mattern* appeared in Berlin and in Paris almost simultaneously. In spite of Antoine's enthusiasm, it can scarcely be said that Hauptmann had any great influence on contemporary French drama. The purely German element in Hauptmann, his poetic inspiration, has not affected French drama in the slightest.

Then again, the Freie Bühne did not perform a single play from the repertory of the Théâtre-Libre, although it did play Zola, the Goncourts, and Becque, all three of them champions of the Théâtre-Libre. Perhaps the German point of view is best explained by Kerr, who wrote in 1894:

> Antoine's Théâtre-Libre is more important for the impulse that it gave than for the productions that were performed there. We owe to him perhaps the finest that we possess to-day. . . . He brought about the establishment of the Freie Bühne to which we must go for the beginning and the cause of the rise of our dramatic art. Antoine's Théâtre-Libre, then, prepared the ground with us, but the flowers which have grown there were engendered by the land itself.

Even if we accept this extremely nationalistic point of view, great is the glory of Antoine.

3. The Théâtre-Libre and English Drama

One of the banalities of modern dramatic criticism has been the assertion that nineteenth-century England produced no great plays. In 1879 Matthew Arnold said:

> In England we have no modern drama at all. Our vast society is not homogeneous enough, not sufficiently united, even any large portion of it, in a common view of life, a common ideal capable of serving as a basis for a modern English drama.

The situation in the eighteen-seventies and eighties was even worse than in Germany. Theatres there were, and actors too, and translations and adaptations from the French, but English plays of the first order were lacking. George Moore and William Archer, who had seen occasional performances of the Théâtre-Libre in Paris, and who had commented on them in English journals, were mainly responsible for the ferment in England during the late eighties.

Why have we not a Théâtre-Libre? [asked Moore]. The innumerable articles which appear in the daily, weekly, and monthly press on the London stage prove the existence of much vague discontent, and that this discontent will take definite shape sooner or later seems possible.

He went on to say that Beerbohm Tree had complained of never meeting anything but conventional and ineffectual plays, but he doubted whether Tree himself would dare to produce a really unconventional play. Moore urged, not a French Théâtre-Libre in England, but an English theatre. He proposed a year's programme composed of the works of Ibsen and Tolstoy, and a group of plays from the Théâtre-Libre, such as *Jacques Damour*, *En Famille*, and *La Mort du duc d'Enghien*. Were he the founder of this revolutionary English theatre, he would apply to the dramatists Jones, Grundy, and Pinero, and to the novelists Meredith, Hardy, and Stevenson, for unconventional plays. The first and almost only qualification would be that the play must be rare. "But are rare plays written in England?" queried the artistic Moore.

William Archer was even more outspoken in his praise of the Théâtre-Libre and in his condemnation of existing conditions. He found the recent drama in England only "a drama of hope," with the native plays of Robertson in the eighteen-sixties, the rise of Irving in the seventies, and the faint promises of Pinero and Jones in the eighties. He realized that regeneration must come from without, and he looked for help from France and the Scandinavian countries. The private performance of Ibsen's *Doll's House* in London in 1889, he pronounced a great event.

The Théâtre-Libre [he wrote in 1891] is not only an established fact, but an artistic force of the first magnitude. We may find in it sheer fanaticism with an impish desire to *épater les bourgeois*, but it is the live theatre of Paris. In the Théâtre-Libre, the curious, subtle, and modern intelligence of Theatropolis has built itself a lordly pleasure house with Antoine for its projector and architect.

No higher praise had come from the pens of the most enthusiastic French critics. Archer felt that if such a theatre were needed in Paris, it was needed a hundred times more in London where the actor-manager reigned supreme. Less sanguine than Moore, he saw that an English Antoine would have to rely almost exclusively on foreign material, as there was no band of daring, brilliant young men in London, where the average intelligence of the patrons of the drama was much lower than that of Paris. In Archer's estimation most English dramatic critics were but theatrical journalists who were most startlingly complacent. "Have we not been for years in a chronic glow of mutual congratulation over the prosperity of the British drama?" he concludes.

And then came Grein, Jacob T. Grein, an expatriated Hollander. "Who is this Dutchman who dares to be dissatisfied with our honest, healthy, comfortable, fat, and flourishing drama?" asked Archer, parodying the storm of criticism that was poured upon the head of this foreign upstart. It was Grein who established in London in 1891 the Independent Theatre. And so England had at last its revolutionary theatre, patterned on a foreign playhouse, introduced by a foreigner, offering as its first play the work of a foreign dramatist, *Ghosts*. Thus for a second time did Ibsen's *Ghosts* serve as the first shot to be fired at the enemy.

In the wake of Antoine, of Paris [tells Grein], I founded the Independent Theatre, the first performance of which elicited no less than five hundred articles, mostly vituperating Ibsen whose *Ghosts* inaugurated the movement, and obtained for me the honorary, if somewhat unflattering, title of the "best-abused man in London." In parenthesis, I should add that this distinction clung to me for many years, that some families closed their doors against me because I had produced an immoral play, and that a well-known journalist, since dead, refused to be present at a banquet if I were invited. It cost me practically ten years of my life to overcome the prejudice created by an undertaking which, even the enemy must admit, has left its mark upon the history of our stage. *Ghosts* was produced on March 9, 1891, under the direction of Mr. Cecil Raleigh, who, together with Mr. George Moore, showed great interest in the little society. Among our first members were George Meredith, Thomas Hardy, H. A. Jones, A. W. Pinero, Mrs. J. R. Green, and many other people of distinction; but in spite of the flourish of adverse trumpets which greeted the birth of the Independent Theatre, the rôle of our members never exceeded 175, and the income was barely £400 a year during the whole of its existence. In fact so poorly was the theatre patronized that in October, 1891, we had only £88 in the bank, and it was with the help of Frank Harris, Frank Danby, and a few others, that I obtained enough money to give a second performance. This was *Thérèse Raquin* of Zola; and again the air was pregnant with abusive language. The next bill was a triple one — a one-act play by Arthur Symons, founded on a story by Frank Harris, Théodore de Banville's charming *Kiss*, translated by John Gray, and George Brandes's famous playlet, *A Visit*, in which Arthur Bourchier and Olga Brandon made a very great success. Even my friend the enemy could not see anything inartistic in this triple bill, and from now the waters became less troubled and the course clearer. I gave four performances a year in those days, and read

about egiht to ten English plays per week — a labour which was but
poorly rewarded by results of any import. In 1892, however, in con-
sequence of a challenge of Mr. George R. Sims, accompanied by a
munificent offer of £100, Mr. George Moore allowed me to produce
his first play, *The Strike at Arlingford*, which created much interest,
and would now I believe be more fully appreciated than in those
days when realism was looked upon as an intruder, and the author
at war with all the critics whom he had denounced in the Pall Mall
Gazette. The greatest and most momentous success, however, which
was achieved by the Independent Theatre occurred in 1893, when
it was my good fortune to obtain from Mr. George Bernard Shaw
the MS. of his first play, *Widowers' Houses*, which immediately
marked him out as a man of destiny. If the Independent Theatre
had done nothing else for the British drama than to give a hearing
to George Bernard Shaw, I contend that it justified its existence and
fulfilled its mission. The rest of the history can be rapidly resumed.
Besides the three original plays named, there were produced, always
under the able direction of Mr. H. de Lange, original works by
Michael Field, by Mrs. Oscar Beringer, by Dr. Todhunter (*The
Black Cat*, which deserves revival), and several plays from the
French, German, and Dutch. In 1894 the well-known novelist Miss
Dorothy Leighton (now Mrs. Ashton Johnson) joined me as co-
director, and substantial financial assistance was forthcoming from
friends who took shares in the Independent Theatre, Ltd. When in
1897 it was found that the Independent Theatre had done its work,
the record showed twenty-two productions in which, including one-
act plays, twenty-six new plays were tried.

Among the very few defenders of the first performance
stand out Moore and Archer. The young critics, Shaw
and Walkley, soon joined the ranks of the independents.
Irving and Tree, who were at first hostile, later loaned
actors. Grein, who, like Antoine, provided the funds of
the first performance out of his own pocket, seems to have
been more of a critic and promoter than a man of the
theatre. He was never militantly aggressive, and was
hampered rather than helped by the fire-eaters Moore
and Shaw. Just as was the case in Germany, there was
much adverse criticism of the Independent Theatre in its

early stage because it produced only foreign plays, but as Grein had stated, no plays of dramatic or literary worth had been received, with the possible exception of Moore's play. But then, Moore, was not a dramatist, and the Independent Theatre had to wait until 1893 before Shaw came and saved the day for England.

Let Shaw tell in his own inimitable way how he turned the trick.

The New Theatre would have never come into existence but for the plays of Ibsen, just as the Bayreuth Festival Playhouse would never have come into existence but for Wagner's Nibelungen tetralogy. . . . Ibsen, then, was the hero of the new departure. It was in 1889 that the first really effective blow was struck by the production of *A Doll's House* by Mr. Charles Charrington and Miss Janet Achurch. Whilst they were taking that epoch-making play around the world, Mr. Grein followed up the campaign in London with his Independent Theatre. It got on its feet by producing Ibsen's *Ghosts;* but the search for native dramatic masterpieces, pursued by Mr. Grein with the ardor and innocence of a foreigner, was so complete a failure that at the end of 1892 he had not produced a single original piece of any magnitude by an English author. In this humiliating national emergency, I proposed to Mr. Grein that he should boldly announce a play by me. Being an extraordinarily sanguine and enterprising man, he took this step without hesitation. I then raked out, from my dustiest pile of discarded and rejected manuscripts, two acts of a play I had begun in 1885, shortly after the close of my novel-writing period, in collaboration with my friend Mr. William Archer.

Mr. Archer has himself described how I proved the most impossible of collaborators. . . . Mr. Archer, perceiving that I had played the fool with his plan and my own theme, promptly disowned me; and the project which neither of us had much at heart, was dropped, leaving me with two abortive acts of an unfinished and condemned play. Exhuming this as aforesaid seven years later, I saw that the very qualities which had made it impossible for ordinary commercial purposes in 1885, might be exactly those needed by the Independent Theatre in 1892. So I completed it by a third act, gave it the farfetched mock-Scriptural title of *Widowers' Houses*, and handed it over to Mr. Grein, who launched it at the public in the Royalty

Theatre with all its original tomfooleries on its head. It made a sensation out of all proportion to its merits or even demerits, and I at once became infamous as a dramatist. . . . I had not achieved a success, but I had provoked an uproar, and the sensation was so agreeable that I resolved to try again.

And that is how Shaw took to writing plays, and, according to Shaw, saved the honor of England. But if you believe that Shaw is a reformer, a preacher, and a propagandist of ideas before he is a dramatist, then you must feel that the English drama was not yet saved.

The Independent Theatre seems to have had a sporadic and nomadic existence, producing only twenty-six plays in seven years. But that it has had considerable influence on English drama is undeniable. It was the germ of the Stage Society, formed some seven years after the Independent Theatre had closed its doors, and it undoubtedly inspired to some extent the Irish Theatre. W. B. Yeats, as well as Archer and Moore, had seen performances of the Théâtre-Libre in Paris. The dramatic situation in England was so bad at the time of the opening of the Independent Theatre that it has taken a longer time than in Germany for the ideals of the Théâtre-Libre to bear fruit. Then again, given the English temperament, changes with them are not sudden and violent. We are seeing to-day the flowering of the ideas of the Independent Theatre in the plays of the contemporary English dramatists. And in the regeneration of English drama, the most potent influences were all foreign, Antione and the Théâtre-Libre, Grein, and Ibsen.

Appendices

APPENDIX A

THE PROGRAMMES OF THE THEATRE–LIBRE

1887

March 30

Mademoiselle Pomme	Comédie-farce en un acte, en prose	Edmond Duranty and Paul Alexis
Un Préfet	Drame en un acte, en prose	Arthur Byl
Jacques Damour	Pièce en un acte, en prose (tirée de la nouvelle d'Émile Zola)	Léon Hennique (Charpentier)
La Cocarde	Comédie en un acte, en prose	Jules Vidal

May 30

La Nuit Bergamasque	Comédie en trois actes, en vers	Émile Bergerat (Lemerre)
En Famille	Pièce en un acte, en prose	Oscar Méténier (Stock)

1887–1888

October 11

Sœur Philomène	Pièce en deux actes, en prose (tirée du roman des Goncourt)	Arthur Byl and Jules Vidal (Vanier)
L'Évasion	Drame en un acte	Villiers de L'Isle-Adam (Stock)

November 11

Belle-Petite	Comédie en un acte, en prose	André Corneau (Stock)
La Femme de Tabarin	Tragi-parade en un acte, en prose	Catulle Mendès (Charpentier)
Esther Brandès	Pièce en trois actes, en prose	Léon Hennique (Stock)

December 23

La Sérénade	Comédie en trois actes, en prose	Jean Jullien (Stock)

Le Baiser	Comédie en un acte, en vers (musique de Paul Vidal)	Théodore de Banville (Charpentier)
Tout pour l'honneur	Drame en un acte (tiré du *Captaine Burle* d'Émile Zola)	Henry Céard (Charpentier)

February 10

La Puissance des ténèbres	Drame en six actes, en prose (traduction Pavlovsky et Méténier)	Léon Tolstoy (Stock)

March 23

La Pelote	Comédie en trois actes, en prose	Paul Bonnetain and Lucien Descaves (Lemerre)
Pierrot assassin de sa femme	Pantomime en un acte (musique de Paul Vidal)	Paul Margueritte [1]
Les Quarts d'heure	Deux tableaux, en prose I. Au mois de mai. II. Entre Frères	Gustave Guiches and Henri Lavedan

April 27

Le Pain du Péché	Drame en deux actes et quatre tableaux, en vers (d'après Aubanel)	Paul Arène (Lemerre)
Matapan	Comédie en trois actes, en vers	Émile Moreau (Ollendorff)

June 15

La Prose	Comédie en trois actes, en prose	Gaston Salandri (Stock)
Monsieur Lamblin	Comédie en un acte, en prose	Georges Ancey (Stock)
La Fin de Lucie Pellegrin	Comédie en un acte, en prose	Paul Alexis (Charpentier)

1888–1889

October 19

Les Bouchers	Drame en un acte, en vers	Fernand Icres (Stock)
Chevalerie rustique	Pièce en un acte, en prose (traduite par Paul Solanges)	Giovanni Verga
L'Amante du Christ	Mystère en un acte, en vers	Rodolphe Darzens (Lemerre)

[1] In *Nos Tréteaux,* published by Les Bibliophiles fantaisistes.

November 5

Rolande   Pièce en cinq actes, en prose   Louis de Gramont   (Stock)

December 10

La Chance de Françoise	Comédie en un acte, en prose	Porto-Riche	(Ollendorff)
La Mort du duc d'Enghien	Drame en trois tableaux, en prose	Léon Hennique	(Stock)
Le Cor fleuri	Féerie en un acte, en vers	Ephraïm Mikhaël	(Stock)

January 15

La Reine Fiammette   Drame en six actes, en vers   Catulle Mendès
(musique de Paul Vidal)   (Charpentier)

January 31

Les Résignés	Pièce en trois actes, en prose	Henry Céard (Charpentier)
L'Echéance	Pièce en un acte, en prose	Jean Jullien [1] (Charpentier)

March 19

La Patrie en Danger   Drame en cinq actes   E. and J. de Goncourt
(Charpentier)

May 2

L'Ancien	Drame en un acte, en vers	Léon Cladel	(Lemerre)
Madeleine	Drame en trois actes, en prose	Émile Zola [2]	
Les Inséparables	Comédie en trois actes, en prose	Georges Alcey	(Stock)

May 31

Le Comte Witold	Pièce en trois actes, en prose	Stanislas Rzewuski (Ollendorff)
Le Cœur révélateur	Pièce en un acte (adaptée d'après la traduction de Tell-Tale Heart de Poe par Charles Baudelaire)	Ernest Laumann
La Casserole	Pièce en un acte, en prose	Oscar Méténier (Stock)

[1] In Le théâtre vivant.
[2] Never published. The novel, Madeleine Férat, was based on this play.

1889–1890

October 21

Dans le Guignol	Prologue en un acte, en prose	Jean Aicard	(Dentu)
Le Père Lebonnard	Pièce en quatre actes, en vers	Jean Aicard	(Dentu)

November 27

Au temps de la ballade	Pièce en un acte, en vers	Georges Bois	(Dentu)
L'École des veufs	Comédie en cinq actes, en prose	Georges Ancey	(Dentu)

January 10

Le Pain d'autrui	Drame en deux actes, en prose (traduit par Armand Ephraïm et Willy Schutz)	Ivan Turgenev	
En Détresse	Pièce en un acte, en prose	Henry Fèvre	(Stock)

February 25

Les Frères Zemganno	Pièce en trois actes, en prose (tirée du livre d'E. de Goncourt)	Paul Alexis and Oscar Méténier	(Charpentier)
Deux tourtereaux	Pièce en un acte, en prose	Paul Ginisty and Jules Guérin	(Dentu)

March 21

Ménages d'artistes	Pièce en trois actes, en prose	Eugène Brieux	(Stock)
Le Maître	Étude de paysans, en trois tableaux	Jean Jullien [1]	(Charpentier)

May 2

Jacques Bouchard	Pièce en un acte, en prose	Pierre Wolff	(Stock)
Une Nouvelle École	Pièce en un acte, en prose	Louis Mullem	(Stock)
La Tante Léontine	Comédie en trois actes, en prose	Maurice Boniface and Edouard Bodin	(Stock)

May 30

Les Revenants	Drame familial en trois actes (traduit du norvégien par Rodolphe Darzens)	Henrik Ibsen	(Stock)
La Pêche	Pièce en un acte, en prose	Henry Céard	

[1] In *Le théâtre vivant*.

June 13

Myrane	Étude dramatique en trois actes, en prose	Émile Bergerat
Les Chapons	Pièce en un acte, en prose	Lucien Descaves and Georges Darien (Stock)

1890–1891
October 29

L'Honneur	Comédie en cinq actes, en prose [1]	Henry Fèvre

November 26

Monsieur Bute	Pièce en trois actes, en prose	Maurice Biollay (Stock)
L'Amant de sa femme	Scènes de la vie parisienne	Aurélien Scholl (Charpentier)
La Belle Opération	Pièce en un acte, en prose	Julien Sermet

December 25

La Fille Élisa	Pièce en trois actes, en prose (tirée du roman d' E. de Goncourt)	Jean Ajalbert (Charpentier)
Conte de Noël	Mystère moderne en deux tableaux, en prose	Auguste Linert

February 26

La Meule	Pièce en quatre actes, en prose	Georges Lecomte (Stock)
Jeune premier	Pièce en un acte, en prose	Paul Ginisty (Stock)

April 27

Le Canard sauvage	Pièce en cinq actes, en prose (traduction d' Armand Ephraïm et Th. Lindenlaub)	Henrik Ibsen

May 26

Nell Horn	Drame en quatre actes et six tableaux, en prose [2]	J.-H. Rosny

[1] Based on the novel by Fèvre.
[2] Based on the novel of the author.

June 8

Leurs filles	Pièce en deux actes, en prose	Pierre Wolff	(Stock)
Les Fourches caudines	Drame en un acte, en prose	Maurice Le Corbeiller	(Ollendorff)
Lidoire	Pièce en un acte, en prose	Georges Courteline	(Flammarion)

July 6

Cœurs simples	Pièce en un acte, en prose	Sutter-Laumann	
Le Pendu	Pièce en un acte, en prose	Eugène Bourgeois	(Stock)
Dans le rêve	Comédie-drame en un acte, en prose	Louis Mullem	(Stock)

1891–1892

October 24

Le Père Goriot	Pièce en cinq actes, en prose (tirée du roman de Balzac)	Adolphe Tarabant

November 30

La Rançon	Comédie en trois actes, en prose	Gaston Salandri	(Stock)
L'Abbé Pierre	Pièce en un acte, en prose	Marcel Prévost	
Un beau soir	Comédie en un acte, en vers	Maurice Vaucaire	(Lemerre)

December 21

La Dupe	Pièce en cinq actes, en prose	Georges Ancey	(Stock)
Son petit cœur	Pièce en un acte, en vers	Louis Marsolleau	

February 2

L'Envers d'une sainte	Pièce en trois actes, en prose	François de Curel	(Stock)
Blanchette	Pièce en trois actes, en prose	Eugène Brieux	(Stock)

March 7

L'Étoile rouge	Pièce en trois actes, en prose	Henry Fèvre	
Seul	Pièce en deux actes, en prose	Albert Guinon	(Ollendorff)

April 29

Simone	Pièce en trois actes, en prose	Louis de Gramont	(Calmann-Lévy)
Les Maris de leurs filles	Pièce en trois actes, en prose	Pierre Wolff	(Stock)

June 8

La Fin du vieux temps	Pièce en trois actes, en prose	Paul Anthelme

June 27

Péché d'amour	Pièce en un acte, en prose	Michel Carré, fils, and Georges Loiseau
Les Fenêtres	Pièce en trois actes, en prose	Jules Perrin and Claude Couturier (Charpentier)
Mélie	Pièce en un acte, en prose (d'après la nouvelle de Jean Reibrach)	Georges Docquois

1892–1893

November 3

Le Grappin	Comédie en trois actes, en prose	Gaston Salandri
L'Affranchie	Comédie en trois actes, en prose	Maurice Biollay (Librairie théâtrale)

November 29

Les Fossiles	Pièce en quatre actes, en prose	François de Curel (Calmann-Lévy)

January 16

Le Ménage Brésile	Pièce en un acte, en prose	Romain Coolus (Charpentier)
Mademoiselle Julie	Tragédie en un acte, en prose (traduite par Charles de Casanove)	Auguste Strindberg (Savine)
A bas le progrès	Bouffonnerie satirique en un acte, en prose	Edmond de Goncourt

February 15

Le Devoir	Pièce en quatre actes, en prose	Louis Bruyerre

March 27

Mirages	Drame en cinq actes, en prose	Georges Lecomte (Calmann-Lévy)

April 27

Valet de cœur	Comédie en trois actes, en prose	Maurice Vaucaire (Charpentier)
Boubouroche	Pièce en deux actes, en prose	Georges Courteline (Charpentier)

May 29

Les Tisserands	Drame en cinq actes, en prose (traduction de Jean Thorel)	Gerhart Hauptmann (Charpentier)

June 12

Ahasvère	Drame en un acte, en prose	Herman Heijermans
Mariage d'argent	Pièce en un acte, en prose	Eugène Bourgeois (Stock)
La Belle au bois rêvant	Comédie en un acte, en vers	Fernand Mazade

1893–1894
November 8

Une Faillite	Pièce en quatre actes, en prose (adaptée par Schürmann et Jacques Lemaire)	Björnstjerne Björnson (Stock)
Le Poète et le financier	Pièce en un acte, en vers	Maurice Vaucaire (Charpentier)

December 26

L'Inquiétude	Pièce en trois actes, en prose	Jules Perrin and Claude Couturier
Amants éternels	Pantomime en trois tableaux (musique d'André Messager)	André Corneau and H. Gerbault

February 1

L'Assomption de Hannele Mattern	Poème de rêve, en deux parties (traduction de Jean Thorel) (musique de Marschalk)	Gerhart Hauptmann (Plon-Nourrit)
En l'attendant	Comédie en un acte, en prose	Léon Roux

February 23

Une Journée parlementaire	Comédie de mœurs, en trois actes, en prose	Maurice Barrès (Charpentier)

April 25

Le Missionnaire	Roman théâtral en cinq tableaux	Marcel Luguet

LAROCHELLE MANAGEMENT

1895

February 14

Elën	Drame en trois actes, en prose (musique d'Auguste Chapuis)	Villiers de l'Isle-Adam (Chamuel)

May 6

L'Argent	Comédie en quatre actes, en prose	Émile Fabre (Stock)

June 13

Grand-papa	Pièce en trois actes, en prose	Claude Berton
Si c'était . . .	Pièce en un acte, en prose	Paul Lheureux

1895–1896
October 24

La Fumée puis la flamme	Pièce en quatre actes, en prose	Joseph Caraguel

December 16

Le Cuivre	Pièce en trois actes, en prose	Paul Adam and André Picard (Ollendorff)

February 10

L'Ame invisible	Pièce en trois actes, en prose	Claude Berton
Mademoiselle Fifi	Drame en un acte, en prose (tiré de la nouvelle de Maupassant)	Oscar Méténier

March 16

Inceste d'âmes	Pièce en cinq actes, en prose	Jean Laurenty and Fernand Hauser
Soldat et mineur	Pièce en un acte, en prose	Jean Malafayde

April 27

La Fille d'Artaban	Drame en un acte, en prose	Alfred Mortier
La Nébuleuse	Pièce en un acte, en prose	Louis Dumur
Dialogue inconnu	Scène en prose	Alfred de Vigny

APPENDIX B

THE PLAYWRIGHTS OF THE THEATRE–LIBRE

Adam, Paul (with André Picard)	*Le Cuivre*
Aicard, Jean	*Dans le Guignol*
	Le Père Lebonnard
Ajalbert, Jean	*La Fille Élisa*
Alexis, Paul	*La Fin de Lucie Pellegrin*
(with Edmond Duranty)	*Mademoiselle Pomme*
(with Oscar Méténier)	*Les Frères Zemganno*
Ancey, Georges	*La Dupe*
	L'École des veufs
	Les Inséparables
	Monsieur Lamblin
Anthelme, Paul	*La Fin du vieux temps*
Arène, Paul	*Le Pain du péché*
Banville, Théodore de	*Le Baiser*
Barrès, Maurice	*Une Journée parlementaire*
Bergerat, Emile	*Myrane*
	La Nuit Bergamasque
Berton, Claude	*L'Ame Invisible*
	Grand-papa
Biollay, Maurice	*L'Affranchie*
	Monsieur Bute
Björnson, Björnstjerne	*Une Faillite*
Bodin, Edouard (with Maurice Boniface)	*La Tante Léontine*
Bois, Georges	*Au temps de la ballade*
Boniface, Maurice (with Edouard Bodin)	*La Tante Léontine*
Bonnetain, Paul (with Lucien Descaves)	*La Pelote*
Bourgeois, Eugène	*Mariage d'argent*
	Le Pendu
Brieux, Eugène	*Blanchette*
	Ménages d'artistes
Bruyerre, Louis	*Le Devoir*
Byl, Arthur	*Un Préfet*
(with Jules Vidal)	*Sœur Philomène*
Caraguel, Joseph	*La Fumée puis la flamme*
Carré, Michel, Fils (with Georges Loiseau)	*Péché d'amour*

Céard, Henry	*La Pêche*
	Les Résignés
	Tout pour l'honneur
Cladel, Léon	*L'Ancien*
Coolus, Romain	*Le Ménage Brésile*
Corneau, André	*Belle-Petite*
(with H. Gerbault)	*Amants éternels*
Courteline, Georges	*Boubouroche*
	Lidoire
Couturier, Claude (with Jules Perrin)	*Les Fenêtres*
	L'Inquiétude
Curel, François de	*L'Envers d'une sainte*
	Les Fossiles
Darien, Georges (with Lucien Descaves)	*Les Chapons*
Darzens, Rodolphe	*L'Amante du Christ*
Descaves, Lucien (with Georges Darien)	*Les Chapons*
(with Paul Bonnetain)	*La Pelote*
Docquois, Georges	*Mélie*
Dumur, Louis	*La Nébuleuse*
Duranty, Edmond (with Paul Alexis)	*Mademoiselle Pomme*
Fabre, Emile	*L'Argent*
Fèvre, Henry	*En Détresse*
	L'Étoile Rouge
	L'Honneur
Gerbault, H. (with André Corneau)	*Amants éternels*
Ginisty, Paul	*Jeune premier*
(with Jules Guérin)	*Deux tourtereaux*
Goncourt, Edmond	*A bas le progrès*
Edmond and Jules	*La Patrie en danger*
Gramont, Louis de	*Rolande*
	Simone
Guérin, Jules (with Paul Ginisty)	*Deux tourtereaux*
Guiches, Gustave (with Henri Lavedan)	*Les Quarts d'heure*
Guinon, Albert	*Seul*
Hauptmann, Gerhart	*L'Assomption de Hannele Mattern*
	Les Tisserands
Hauser, Fernand (with Jean Laurenty)	*Inceste d'âmes*
Heijermans, Herman	*Ahasvère*
Hennique, Léon	*Esther Brandès*
	Jacques Damour
	La Mort du duc d'Enghien

Ibsen, Henrik	*Le Canard sauvage*
	Les Revenants
Icres, Fernand	*Les Bouchers*
Jullien, Jean	*L'Echéance*
	Le Maître
	La Sérénade
Laumann, Ernest	*Le cœur révélateur*
Laurenty, Jean (with Fernand Hauser)	*Inceste d'âmes*
Lavedan, Henry (with Gustave Guiches)	*Les Quarts d'heure*
Lecomte, Georges	*La Meule*
	Les Mirages
Le Corbeiller, Maurice	*Les Fourches caudines*
Lheureux, Paul	*Si c'était . . .*
Linert, Auguste	*Conte de Noël*
Loiseau, Georges	*Péché d'amour*
Luguet, Marcel	*Le Missionnaire*
Malafayde, Jean	*Soldat et mineur*
Margueritte, Paul	*Pierrot assassin de sa femme*
Marsolleau, Louis	*Son petit cœur*
Mazade, Fernand	*La Belle au bois rêvant*
Mendès, Catulle	*La Femme de Tabarin*
	La Reine Fiammette
Méténier, Oscar	*La Casserole*
	En Famille
	Mademoiselle Fifi
(with Paul Alexis)	*Les Frères Zemganno*
Mikhaël, Ephraïm	*Le Cor fleuri*
Moreau, Émile	*Matapan*
Mortier, Alfred	*La Fille d'Artaban*
Mullem, Louis	*Dans le rêve*
	Une nouvelle école
Perrin, Jules (with Claude Couturier)	*Les Fenêtres*
	L'Inquiétude
Picard, André (with Paul Adam)	*Le Cuivre*
Porto-Riche, Georges de	*La Chance de Françoise*
Prévost, Marcel	*L'Abbé Pierre*
Rosny, J.-H.	*Nell Horn*
Roux, Léon	*En l'attendant*
Rzewuski, Stanislas	*Le Comte Witold*
Salandri, Gaston	*Le Grappin*
	La Prose
	La Rançon

Scholl, Aurélien	*L'Amant de sa femme*
Sermet, Julien	*La Belle Opération*
Solanges, Paul	*Chevalerie rustique*
Strindberg, August	*Mademoiselle Julie*
Sutter-Laumann	*Cœurs simples*
Tabarant, Adolphe	*Le Père Goriot*
Tolstoy, Leo	*La Puissance des ténèbres*
Turgenev, Ivan	*Le Pain d'autrui*
Vaucaire, Maurice	*Le Poète et le financier*
	Un beau soir
	Valet de cœur
Verga, Giovanni	*Chevalerie rustique*
Vidal, Jules	*La Cocarde*
(with Arthur Byl)	*Sœur Philomène*
Vigny, Alfred de	*Dialogue inconnu*
Villiers de l'Isle-Adam	*Elën*
	L'Évasion
Wolff, Pierre	*Jacques Bouchard*
	Leurs filles
	Les Maris de leurs filles
Zola, Émile	*Madeleine*

APPENDIX C

THE ACTORS OF THE THEATRE–LIBRE

(Important ones appear in capitals)

Messieurs:
- Albert
- AMYOT
- D'Argis
- D'ARQUILLIÈRE, ALEXANDRE
- Aventure
- Baillet
- BERTIN
- BRÉVERN
- BURGUET, HENRI
- Camis
- Campbell
- Candès
- Capoul, Victor
- Castillan
- CERNAY
- CHAMOISEL
- Charlot
- Charpentier
- Chastaignié
- CHRISTIAN, LÉON
- Clerget (Paul Cléry)
- Collé
- Cosmydor
- Couchy
- Damon
- DAMOYE
- Dancourt
- Darney
- Debel
- Defrance
- DELIGNY
- Delorme

Messieurs:
- Demeyer
- DEPAS
- Désiré
- Desmard
- Desmarets
- Destrey
- Deval, Abel
- Dornans
- DORVAL
- Dowe
- Dubarry
- DUJEU
- Dulnard
- Dupont
- Durtal, Henri
- Edmond, Paul
- ETIÉVANT
- Fechter
- Férou
- Fleury-Fontès
- Franck, Paul
- Gandiot
- Gauley, Armand
- GÉMIER, FIRMIN
- Georges
- Gerès
- GODEFROY
- GRAND, GEORGE
- Guenin
- Guichard
- Hanryot
- Herlaine

Messieurs:
Hermann
Hérouin
JANVIER, JEAN-LOUIS (Nugeyre)
Kanne
Kéraval
Krauss, Henri
Lambert
Larchal
LAROCHE
Larochelle
LAUDNER
Lauras
LAURY
Lérand
Leubas
Levanz
Lucque
Ludi
LUGNÉ-POE (Philipon) (Leroy)
MARCEL, EDMOND
Margueritte, Paul
Mayer, Edmond
MAYER, HENRY
Mercier
Méré
MÉVISTO
MICHELEZ
MORIÈRE
Moritz
Mornand
Osip
Pausader
Pelio
Petit
PINSARD
Pinsard fils
Poggi
PONS-ARLÈS
Presle

Messieurs:
Rablet
Rami
Raymond, Émile
RENARD
Renaudot
Rey
Ricouard
Rosambeau
Séruzier, Henri
Séverin-Mars
Severino
Taillade
Tandier
Tervil
Thiel
TIMBOT (Tinbot?)
VERSE
Viart-Burguet
Viterbo
Wil (Will?)
Mesdames:
Achard, Marguerite
Alix
André
D'Armières
D'Arthien
AUBRY, MARIE
BADY, BERTHE (Heldy)
Bailly, Marcelle
BARNY
Bartelet
Belly
Béraldi
Béro, Any
Bernard, Alice
Berthier, petite Jeanne
Bérys, Yvonne
BESNIER
Bouchetal

Mesdames:
Bouffé
Bréval
Brienne
CARDINAL, EVE
Carlix
Caron, Marguérite
Celny
Clem, Annette
COLAS, LUCE
Colomb, Francine
Courty
Dallet
Darnay
Daubrives
DEFRESNES, MARIE
Delpré, Odette
DENEUILLY
Devèze, petite Marie
Dorny
DORSY, LUCIENNE
Duhamel, petite
DULAC, JEANNE
FARNA, ALICE
DE FEHL, ODETTE
Fériel
Fernande
Ferville
FLEURY, GABRIELLE
FRANCE, LOUISE
FRANCK
GARNIERI
Gay, Suzanne
Gerfaut
Guimont
HELLEN
HENRIOT
Henry, Henriette
Isaac, Mary
Jolly, Blanche

Mesdames:
Justin
Laporte
LAURE, MARIE
Laurent, Antonia
LEFRANÇAIS
Lemorié
Léonce, Lucy
Lerou, Emilie
Léry, Jeanne
Maggini
Mallet, Félicia
Manvel, Lucy
Mario
MARLEY, SUZANNE
MARTIAL, RÉGINE
Mary, Suzanne
Massy
MÉRÉANE
MEURIS
Miramon
Mona
NAU, EUGÉNIE
Palmat
Parfait, petite Laurence
PERROT, IRMA
Pinson, Julia
Poraye
Raki, Gabrielle
Raymonde, petite
Renozy
Reynold, Berthe
Rolland, Marguerite
SAVELLI
Schatz, petite Suzanne
Schmitt, Rose
Sigall(e)
Sindt
De Sivry
Spinoy

Mesdames:
Suger
Sylly
Sylviac
Tassilly
Thabuis
THEVEN
Valdey, Marcelle
Varly

Mesdames:
VERNET, NANCY
Veryna
Villetard, Amélie
VINET
Walter, petite
Wolbel
Zapolska
Zobel, Annie

BIBLIOGRAPHICAL NOTE

Le Théâtre Libre. *Saisons 1887 à 1890.* Brochure, 37 pp.

Le Théâtre Libre. *Mai 1890.* Brochure, 186 pp.

Le Théâtre Libre. *Octobre 1891.* Brochure, 89 pp.

Le Théâtre Libre. *Saisons 1893–1894.* Brochure, 26 pp.

(These four brochures were privately printed by the Théâtre-Libre.)

Rodolphe Darzens. *Le Théâtre Libre Illustré* (1889–1890). Paris, 1890.

Adolphe Thalasso. *Le Théâtre Libre.* Paris, 1909.

Antoine. *"Mes Souvenirs"* sur le Théâtre-Libre.

Forty volumes of newspaper clippings on the Théâtre-Libre, in the archives of M. Antoine.

Index